AN ANGLESEY
ANTHOLOGY

An Anglesey
Anthology
by Dewi Roberts

ISBN: 0-86381-566-9

Cover illustration: The National Library of Wales

Cover design: Smala, Caernarfon

First published in 1999 by Gwasg Carreg Gwalch,
12 Iard yr Orsaf, Llanrwst, Wales LL26 0EH.
☎ (01492) 642031
Printed and published in Wales.

Dewi Roberts lives in a Denbighshire village and this is his eighth book. His other works include *Visitors Delight, A Clwyd Anthology, The Land of Old Renown, Christmas in Wales, Both Sides of the Border* and *The Old Villages of Denbighshire and Flintshire*. He is a member of the Academi and is active as a reviewer and speaker on literary and historical topics.

for Sir Kyffin Williams

Comments on *An Anglesey Anthology*

This book is an astonishingly comprehensive and entertaining portrait of one of the most fascinating islands in Europe, with contributions from scores of its most distinguished visitors and residents. It will not only be a perfect travelling companion, but also a permanently invaluable handbook to the history and culture of Anglesey.

Jan Morris

Human beings, like flora and fauna, flourish best when they cherish their habitat. Back in the seventeenth century the antiquary Henry Rowlands considered his Mona a favoured isle and the evidence of this wide-ranging collection suggests that its inhabitants considered themselves 'favoured' to be living on it. They expect visitors and newcomers to share their enthusiasm and these well chosen poems and prose extracts demonstrate, with one or two notable exceptions, that they usually do.

Emyr Humphreys

Contents

Acknowledgements

We would like to thank the following authors, owners of copyright, publishers, literary agents and executors for permission to reprint the poems and prose extracts included in this anthology.

Jan Morris for 'The Centre of Resistance' from *The Matter of Wales*

Kyffin Williams and Gomer for 'Fairyland' from *Across the Straits*

Gwynedd Archives for 'Transportation' from *Australians from Wales* by the late Lewis Lloyd

Gwynedd Archives for 'Rivalry' from *Packet to Ireland* by the late M. Ellis Williams

Michael Senior for 'The Conquest' and 'Penmon' from *Portrait of North Wales* (Gwasg Carreg Gwalch)

Dilys Gater for 'The Rothsay Castle Tragedy' from *Historic Shipwrecks in Wales* (Gwasg Carreg Gwalch)

Manon and Catherine Eames for two items by the late Aled Eames – 'Island to Island' from *Ships and Seamen of Anglesey* (Anglesey Antiquarian Society) and 'Learning Their Seamanship' from *Shrouded Quays* (Gwasg Carreg Gwalch)

Professors William Tydeman and Alun Jones for 'Grand and Striking' from *A Pedestrian Tour of North Wales* by Joseph Hucks (University of Wales Press)

Random House UK Limited for 'Like Robinson Crusoe' from *Francis Kilvert's Diary*

Gwasg Gee and Son (Denbigh) Ltd for 'An English Air' from *Michael Farraday in Wales* edited by Dafydd Tomos

Thomas Roberts, of the Department of Manuscripts at the University of Wales, Bangor, and the Anglesey Antiquarian Society for extracts from the Bulkeley Diaries (Anglesey Antiquarian Society)

Emyr Price for 'Great Men of Anglesey' from *Lord Cledwyn of Penrhos* (The University of Wales Institute of Research)

Dr Christopher Madoc-Jones for 'Beaumaris Grammar School' by the late Geraint Madoc-Jones from the Transactions of the Anglesey Antiquarian Society

Dr A.D. Carr for 'An Evolving Landscape' from *Medieval Anglesey* (Anglesey Antiquarian Society Transactions)

Tony Conran for 'Winter at Llanddwyn' and 'Sending A Harrier to Llaneilian' from the as yet unpublished *A Gwynedd Symphony*

Emyr Humphreys for 'In Love With An Island', reproduced from 'The Spectator'

Peter Gruffydd for 'No Passage Landward' and 'Plas Newydd, by God' originally published in 'The New Welsh Review'

Huw Jones for his own translation of 'Din Llugwy'

Bryan Aspden for 'Pentrepella – Kyffin Williams'

Gladys Mary Coles for 'The Shock' from *The Glass Island* (Duckworth)

Sally Roberts Jones for 'Wreck of the Royal Charter', 'Language Protest, Llangefni' and 'William Evans, Llangefni'

Fiona Owen for 'Bonfire Night', which first appeared in 'Poetry Wales' and 'Hay-making in Capel Gwyn'

Richard Poole for his previously unpublished poem 'Interlude at Traeth Bychan'

John Hywel for 'Bone Setters' by the late W. Hywel Jones from the Anglesey Antiquarian Society Transactions

Teresa Francis for 'Gratitude', an extract from a letter

Glenda Beagan for 'Manikin' from *Vixen* (Honno)

Marianne Jones for *Change,* which originally appeared in 'The New Welsh Review'

Wendy Lloyd Jones for *A Keepsake for Miss Adams*

Alun Owen for 'The Whalers of Anglesey' from *The Whalers of Anglesey* (Gwynedd Archives)

Professor Dafydd Johnson for his translation of Iolo Goch's *Praise of Tudur Fychan's Sons* which originally appeared in *Iolo Goch: Poems* (Gwasg Gomer)

Dr Rachel Bromwich for her translation of Dafydd ap Gwilym's 'A Prayer to St Dwynwen' from *Dafydd ap Gwilym: Poems* (Gwasg Gomer)

Professor Joseph P. Clancy for his translation of T. Gwynn Jones' poem 'Penmon' from *Twentieth Century Welsh Poems* (Gomer)

Tony Conran for his translation of Goronwy Owen's 'The Wish' from *Welsh Verse* (Seren)

Roland Mathias for 'Porth Cwyfan'

Gareth Alban Davies for his translation of his own poem 'Huw Owen, Gwenynog, Anglesey'

Jane Edwards for 'Blind Date' in a translation by Derec Llwyd Morgan which originally appeared in 'The Penguin Book of Welsh Short Stories' edited by Alun Richards

R.S. Thomas for 'A Holyhead Childhood' from *The Paths Gone By* included in Selected Prose (Seren) edited by Sandra Anstey

Steve Griffiths and Seren for 'Patchworks' and 'Out of a descended generation'

Acknowledgements also to the National Library of Wales for permission to reproduce the print 'Pride' by T. Picken on the front cover.

14

Introduction

Today's tourists who drive over the Menai Straits each year in such large numbers are often lured by brochure promises. They visit the tourist venues featured in promotional literature, spend Summer days on the beaches and have a generally pleasant time.

But I wonder how many of these visitors are aware of what a very rich region Anglesey is both culturally and historically?

I was not myself fully aware of this until I undertook the labour of love which editing this anthology entailed.

The island has contributed to Welsh history in a unique way and it is not therefore surprising that historical topics occupy so much of the space here in one way or another.

The earliest piece of historical interest in the anthology is by a visitor. The account by Tacitus of the Roman invasion of the island refers to 'the fearful appearance of the Britons' on the far side of the Straits. The Romans were 'struck with astonishment'.

When Giraldus Cambrensis came in 1188 he had an eye for the curious and it is a sense of the inquisitive which characterises a good deal of the writing of literary tourists in the eighteenth and nineteenth centuries. For much of this period notions of the picturesque determined what they found aesthetically appealing. It may come as a surprise to find this ideal being extended to a polluted copper mine, but visiting Amlwch, William Bingley describes 'a vast and tremendous chasm' which 'excited the most sublime ideas'.

It would be difficult to imagine a travel writer of today going into raptures about an aluminium plant, or even a nuclear power station!

Holyhead and Holy Island have always been important to travellers to Ireland. The early Christian pilgrims crossed Anglesey and sailed from here, and as the centuries went by an increasing number of people of all kinds followed the same route. In the eighteenth century Jonathan Swift travelled, rather reluctantly, through north Wales on his many journeys between Dublin and London and has left us his disgruntled impressions.

The poetry input is strong and includes items by such prominent early poets as Iolo Goch, Dafydd ap Gwilym and Gwalchmai and ranges over the centuries to embrace contemporary voices including Steve Griffiths, Sally Roberts Jones, Richard Poole, and Gareth Alban Davies. The selection of prose writers on a very miscellaneous range of topics adds impetus to my belief that Ynys Môn has produced as fine a body of literature, at least, as any other region of Wales. Which other region could one focus on for anthology material to come up with such disparate names as Dr Johnson, Goronwy Owen, Thomas Pennant, and John Wesley as well as such twentieth century luminaries as R.S. Thomas, Kyffin Williams, Emyr Humphreys and Jan Morris?

I have included not only English writing but also a good deal of Welsh-language material in translation.

But it is not only the well known who are represented here, for I have also drawn on the writing of certain aspiring writers, most of whom live on the island, and whose work seems to me well worthy of inclusion. Much of their work is making its first appearance in print.

Although many of my inclusions are self explanatory, I have included certain introductory notes where these appeared to me to be appropriate.

I end with the deep sense of pride which seems to be such a notable feature among the island people. Goronwy Owen's name is synonymous with the region and when he was living in ill-fated exile in Virginia he longed for nothing more than to be back among his own people on Ynys Môn. Let him have the final word:

> I'd go back to my father's country,
> Live respected, not lavish nor meagerly
> In sunlit Môn, a land most lovely, with
> Cheerful men in it full of ability.

Dewi Roberts

Prologue: In love with an island

On the mainland side of the Menai suspension bridge which is now the single slender entry into Anglesey, there is a bold legend which reads *Môn Mam Cymru*. This is our county motto and it means 'Anglesey the mother of Wales'. In any context this is a formidable responsibility. Geologically, it was first undertaken millions of years ago and we are told that because the island stood firm, mountains were born out of the dome-shaped massif which the tourist calls Snowdonia and the native, Eryri. Geography, which is juster than history, still allows us on the island the best view of those myth-making mountains.

This island on which I live was the last refuge of the Druids, that mysterious mandarin priesthood that seems to have administered the lost Celtic world that stretched from the Alps to the Irish Sea. This is where the grim pursuit ended and those inhuman robots the Romans conducted their slaughter in silence while the female dependants of the solemn order fled shrieking into the dark oak forests. Today the island looks bare and small but in prehistoric times, before the Romans and the Druids, it was a wooded continent. Adventurous tribes arriving on the west coast from the Iberian peninsula or from Ireland would wander into the woods and be confronted by astonished beaker folk who had made the long journey slowly overland from the Rhine and the Lowlands. They must have stared at each other with the same unease and suspicion which we see today when a monoglot farm labourer resentfully empties the summer dustbins of a caravan occupied by a cheerful mono with a different glot who has brought his family and his outboard motor boat all the way from Walsall or St Helens.

Throughout its long history Môn (the name 'Anglesey' is inappropriate except for titles and railway timetables) has always had these two functions: a refuge and a meeting-place; and to be thoroughly unkind about it has regularly made a mess of both. Proudly detached from the mainland, it is exceedingly vulnerable from the sea. Oddly enough it was many centuries before this elementary strategic fact bore in upon the ox-like consciousness of the English, Norman and Plantagenet kings. (We can't count the Vikings, bent on plunder rather than conquest.) Throughout the Middle Ages, Môn was the granary of independent Wales. It had to be ravaged before the princes could be brought to their knees.

Less than half a dozen miles away from me as I write is the traditional home of the Tudor family. They served the Princes of Wales with fidelity and distinction and they were well rewarded. Somewhere above the shifting sand-dunes of Aberffraw those ancient princes held their court, and to that court the story-tellers would come from all over Wales and the borders, to reassure them that in the fullness of time they would be restored to their rightful place and the crown of Arthur would once more rule from the throne of Britain. The Tudors proved themselves the more attentive listeners. Long after their first masters had been crushed they fished successfully in troubled waters.

An island like this one exists in order to give birth to poets as well as mountains. The past, like the western sea, never stops lapping its shores, giving the most simple men illusions of grandeur. Môn has its own annual eisteddfod held in different parts of the island every Whitsuntide. Last year it came to our parish because the date was also the two hundredth anniversary of the death of Goronwy Owen in faraway Virginia, and he was born here, a small man with a great talent and an unfortunate love of the bottle. In his chequered career he was an eighteenth century Dylan Thomas, as fine a letter writer as he was a poet. A handful of his bewildered American descendents were firmly initiated into the Order of Anglesey Bards by our aged archdruid who in his younger days earned his living as a gamekeeper. They were mostly natives of Mobile, Alabama and there was no means of knowing whether it was our Whitsun weather or our rituals that made them shiver. Certainly their stay was brief. They had business elsewhere. Perhaps they were wise to leave. It is difficult to live in Anglesey for long and not to risk becoming some sort of a poet.

Our poets come in all shapes and sizes. There was John Evans, for example. who cherished the strange ambition of marrying the widowed Queen Victoria. He was known as Bardd Cocos (the Cockle Poet) and children still recite his immortal lines to the lions which guard – rather ineffectively as it turns out – the Britannia Tubular Bridge.

'Four fat lions without any hair
Two over here and two over there.'

His dynastic ambitions were not as insane as all that: had not Owen Tudor of Penmynydd managed to marry a royal widow?

From the field above this house I can see Moelfre which was always a fishing village. Now, alas, it is more of a holiday resort: but the lifeboat is still famous for saving lives at sea. Over a century ago Charles Dickens came bustling up from London to praise the parson and the fisherfolk of Moelfre for their rescue and recovery work at the wreck of 'The Royal Charter'. And more than a century before that, Lewis Morris wrote a savage poem to denounce the wreckers of Grigyll (on the other side of the island). The three Morris brothers (from this side) remain one of the wonders of Anglesey: antiquarians, scientists, surveyors, botanists, poets and above all great letter-writers. Their collected works read as though James Boswell had written the Paston letters.

In the nineteenth century the normal island alternative to being a poet was to be a preacher. Anglesey threw up ('nurtured' perhaps would be a happier expression) so many eloquent men that it developed an oratorical style of its own (Dawn Môn). A Tory Methodist named John Elias took the island in hand and built or caused to be built more than a chapel a year for the rest of his working life. Popularly known as Anglesey's Methodist pope, he became an outstanding figure of Welsh nonconformist life and created that mould of eloquence and administrative ability that made, among many others, David Lloyd George. Curiously enough this island is also the birthplace of the only Welshman to get anywhere near being elected Pope: Owen Lewis, bishop of Cassano and founder of the so-called English College in Rome.

'So-called' betrays that after five years residence I have caught the prevailing island disease. It has, as far as I know, no Latin name: but the outstanding symptom is an insane affection for the place, which spills over into inanimate objects and turns even a broken gate into a relic. The disease is not new. To return to the poets for a moment, among the 'Hail to thee' subjects Môn ranks with Caesar, Hitler and the skylark. In its milder forms it makes otherwise harmless-looking men turn their homes into museums which they open at impossible hours to visitors who can produce fervently written testimonials to the sincerity of their interest. Roadmen (I know at least two) write splendid books which ostensibly are about their experiences in the Great war or working on paddle steamers on the Mississippi, but are in fact paeans of unrestrained praise to the island of their birth. Farm labourers work themselves to a shadow all their lives to be able to buy smallholdings that consist chiefly of rocks and gorse in order to feel that part of the island at least belongs to them.

This mysterious disease must account for the universal detestation of caravan sites, especially if they belong to someone else. On village street corners and at crossroads the laws of conversation have long ago decreed that contractors from Manchester (or anywhere else) should not be allowed to carry off headlands and other wellknown landmarks. It has been agreed that monster caravans should not be allowed to sneak across the bridge at three o'clock in the morning and that all builders – spec, council or government – should be compelled to use slate only for roofing material, and that farmers large and small should receive subsidies to enable them to double their labour force and solve the island's unemployment problem. It was the general view that pylons should be banned and all cables routed through sewers that passed unobtrusively through our network of marshes, Resolutions to reopen the old railway lines were passed by acclamation. They could be run as a tourist attraction, provide free transport for the islanders and relieve congestion on the roads.

Alas, democracy does not work in this old-world way. The headlands are disappearing, the pylons are multiplying almost as fast as the nasty tiled roofs and the farmers are reduced to turning their fields into caravan sites without even being obliged to camouflage them like wartime aerodromes.

Can you really blame us for our hostility to such things as caravan sites, speedboats, yachting clubs, racing cars, gift shops, cafeterias, amusement arcades, car parks and massive public conveniences which have taken over every available inch of the coastline from the shrine of St Seiriol to the shrine of St Cybi (or in signpost language, from Beaumaris to Holyhead)? What can we do from June to September except retreat inland to glower malevolently at the invaders enjoying themselves and helping giant organisations like Rio Tinto and Shell and the Central Electricity Board and their allies in the London government to pollute our sacred shores for ever more? Up in our cottage bedrooms and granite towers we dream of myths more potent than Branwen who taught a starling to speak: and these will enable us to put a language barrier across the bridge and buy back the soul of the island.

Emyr Humphreys (1970)

Topography:

The Character of Anglesey

There is something remarkable in the character of Anglesey. The bold mountains of Wales come to an abrupt fall at the Menai Straits, and thence the island stretches west in low undulation rising nowhere to any considerable elevation, and scored across with depressions from north to south, feeble and imperfect replicas of the Menai Straits. One is the furrow occupied by the Malldraeth morass and sands, but this does not cut completely across the island. The other is more thorough; it severs Holy Island from the main body of Môn, but it is so narrow that it has been bridged at Penybont and the railway crosses it on a causeway at Valley.

Anglesey does not impress the visitor as being so fertile as has been supposed. There are long stretches of morass and moor strewn with pools. But perhaps Môn was first called the 'Mother of Wales' because to it, as to a mother's lap, retreated the Cymry when beaten, wounded, and sore before their oppressors. If so, it soon ceased to be their place of refuge, but formed a *point d'appui* for their enemies, whence to strike at them from the rear.

Mona, as already said, does not present us with very striking scenery, except on the coast, but it teems with interest in other ways. It is dotted with monuments of the primeval inhabitants – cromlechs and meini-hirion (the plural of maen-hir). It possesses very well preserved camps of the Gwyddyl invaders. It was first the sanctuary and school of the Druids, and after that, of their spiritual successors, the Saints. The slope of Mona towards the east is well timbered and studded with mansions, the park of Plas Newydd, the residence of the Marquess of Anglesey, Plas Llanfair, and the palace of the Bishop of Bangor. This prelate had his residence near the Cathedral, but this has been sold, and a lordly mansion has been given to him on the Straits, where he can turn his back on his Anglesey clergy, and say to the rest, 'Between us and you there is a great gulf fixed.'

S. Baring Gould: 'A Book of North Wales' (1905)

Night and Morning

One night of tempest I arose and went
Along the Menai shore on dreaming bent;
The wind was strong, and savage swung the tide,
And the waves blustered on Caernarfon side.

But on the morrow, when I passed that way,
On Menai shore the hush of heaven lay;
The wind was gentle and the sea a flower,
And the sun slumbered on Caernarfon tower.

Anon: 16th century; translated from the Welsh

Magical, Mystical Môn

Windy Isle where mills once ground the corn.
Golden, rippling acres flow towards the
beckoning boundaries of the sea.
Breezes whisper age-old incantations
as the *Stones* stand erect and weather-worn.
Ghosts of past and present mingle,
drawn by the whispering hypnotic hills.
Rocks call from their depths –
like mermaids lure an unsuspecting sailor to his doom.

By chance I came across a small stone church –
hidden down a winding, unknown lane.
Tall trees formed shady sanctuary,
the stillness pierced only by raucous rooks,
disturbed at their summit from evening meditation.
Echoes of hymns spanning centuries
drifted faintly through the slightly opened door.
Slowly stepping inside, dark and dim the interior,
illuminated slightly by the sun's last rays,
glowed leaded windows – stained with saintly smiles
and ancient situations.
Lords, ladies, farmhands and serving maids all knelt here –
each seeking their own measure of absolution
from a raging God who filled them with His fire
on the high and stony pulpit,

to a more sensitive and silent God,
that sought them as they tilled the fields
and shepherded their flocks on grassy, rocky slopes.

Keeping her secrets, the sea circles.
Calm at times, then suddenly becoming a ferocious thing.
Storms rage – battering her boundaries.
Ghostly lanterns drew many a ship onto these rocks,
as eager hands pillaged cargoes, subsidizing meager means.
Hastening home as the galloping hooves of excise men's horses
were heard approaching the scene.
Magical, Mystical Môn – your winds and sea still weave their spell,
and the *Stones* call out to us to stay.

Iona James

An Evolving Landscape

. . . the Welsh landscape cannot be dismissed out of hand as a world of mountains, sheep-walks and upland pastures. Nor can anyone delude himself that landscape is a mere natural phenomenon, untouched by human hand; since Neolithic times man has shaped his environment and he does so still. Even if the term 'man-made' as applied to landscape brings to mind the part played by such men as Capability Brown in the eighteenth century, the fact remains that most landscape is, to a greater or lesser degree, man-made. It has been said of a later period that 'the ravaging of Parys Mountain financed the landscape gardening of Llysdulas' and this illustrates the process of change very clearly. The devastation wrought by copper-mining on Mynydd Parys is familiar to all and if the glory of Llysdulas has departed, the grounds at Plas Newydd were probably paid for from the same source. But neither mines nor grounds were to be seen in the middle ages and that sums up the argument. Landscape is dynamic; it has changed, is changing and will go on changing.

The basis of the landscape is land. Anglesey is an island. It covers an area of 290 square miles or 175,811 acres and is approximately square in shape, measuring 23 miles from south-east to north-west and 21 miles from north-east to south-west. It is separated from the mainland of Britain by the Menai Straits, which are some fifteen miles long and a smaller island, Holy Island or Ynys Cybi, lies to the west of it. Off the coast are various small islands and reefs. It is undulating and low; the grandeur and drama of Snowdonia will be sought in vain, although some of the finest views of the mountains are to be had from across the Menai Straits. In fact, the contrast with mainland Gwynedd is extreme; there is more low-lying land in Anglesey than in any other of the historic counties of Wales and the highest point is only 720 feet above sea-level. In geological terms the island is very old and it includes some of the oldest rock formations in Britain. There are no large rivers but there are many small ones along with a number of lakes and marshy tracts. Drainage is mainly from north-east to south-west and this alignment is also to be seen in the Menai Straits and in the geological fault which runs from Red Wharf Bay to Malltraeth Marsh and which forms a natural division between the region known as Sir Fôn Fach to the south and that known as Sir Fôn Fawr to the north.

Much of the present-day landscape is the result of changes which came about in the nineteenth century. The island is linked to the mainland by two bridges, one built by Thomas Telford and completed in 1826 and the other built by Robert Stephenson in 1850 to carry the Chester and Holyhead Railway. Telford also built a new road linking his bridge with Holyhead, while the railway takes a more southerly route. The largest town by far is the port of Holyhead; next to it comes the former county town, Llangefni, followed by Amlwch, Menai Bridge and Beaumaris. Other semi-urban settlements have developed, often as a result of the holiday industry and there has been a great deal of residential development along the Menai Straits. Nucleated villages do exist but these are far fewer than one would expect to find in an English county. The outstanding example of the impact of industry on the landscape is Mynydd Parys which has still not recovered from the pollution caused by copper-mining at the end of the eighteenth century, but there is no shortage of other industrial remains. The twentieth century has brought more industry, particularly a large aluminium smelter near Holyhead and a nuclear power station at Wylfa and the presence of the latter, along with the universal availability of electric power, has brought high-voltage power lines and the pylons which carry them; these, too, are part of an evolving landscape.

A.D. Carr: 'Medieval Anglesey' (1982)

A Favoured Isle

Anglesey, anciently called Mona, is an island seated in a temperate air, enlivene'd by a benign sun, and enrich'd with good and beautiful soil.

Henry Rowlands: 'Mona Antiqa Restaurata' (1723)

24

Isolation

Anglesey is often supposed to be the least interesting of Welsh counties. The *Monites*, however, warmly repudiate this remark, and use the bardic appellation, 'Mon mam Cymru' (Mona, the mother of Wales). This designation was probably based on an old belief that the soil of the island was so fertile as to raise a sufficient quantity of corn for the maintenance of the population of the whole of Wales. It is more probable that the Isle of Mona and the Isle of Man derive their names from *Mon*, which means, 'what is isolated', 'separate'. The English name was bestowed on it in 818 or 819 by the Saxon king who subdued it, calling it the Isle of the Angles or English. The Menai Straits present one of the finest views in Wales. The population is small and scattered, and Calvinistic Methodism has a strong hold throughout this county.

David Young: The Origin and History of the Methodists in Wales' (1893)

'An English Air'

Wednesday, July 28th, 1819
We left Caernarvon this morning in company with our Essex friends and went in a boat up the Menai Straits. The width of the channel varies in different places being near Caernarvon a mile and a half across at other places not a quarter of a mile. Herons, Cormorants and other birds were fishing here and there up the straits. The scenery was pretty and our row an excellent variety amongst the other modes of conveyance we have at different times adopted. It saved us little fatigue and was on that account agreeable as we had 17 miles to walk afterwards. Near the Bangor Ferry preparations are making for the new hanging bridge over the Straits projected by Mr Telford. It will be – feet long and consist of one arch. The boat put ashore on the Anglesey side of the Straits when we had reached the Ferry and we here bade our friends a final farewell. They were going to Bangor and from there rapidly home. They had added much to our amusement and pleasure in various places by their company and they certainly, for their kindness and good nature, deserve our heartiest acknowledgements and best wishes.

We left the ferry in good plight for Amlwch ignorant of the road but inquiring everywhere. We went very much about and the day was extremely hot but we nevertheless fagged on without any rest or refreshments towards our goal Amlwch.

This island differs very much in appearance from the other parts of

Wales. It is more cultivated and peopled and a much larger number of habitations are sprinkled about it. There is a sort of English air over the place and to a Londoner this seems more than the case from the comparative flatness of the country and as there is, or at least there was, a continual mist throughout the day hanging over the shores of the island, it hid the sea from our view.

Michael Faraday: 'Tour in Wales: 1819' from
'Michael Farraday in Wales' edited by Dafydd Tomos

'A Hanging Festoon'

Of all the tour accounts of Wales in the nineteenth century the one from which a passage is extracted below must surely rank as among the most eccentric. There is a great deal of dramatic, colourful and exaggerated dialogue in the book, as here.

'Dang it, master, what's that!' cried Clavileno; 'look, sir, what a sweep! what a bow! 'tisnt a rainbow, because it curves downwards instead of upwards – what a hanging *festoon*! – Just observe the two great towers, like sharp pointed pyramids! – and see the curved somethings suspended from the tops of them! – and the arches, oh see! – 'Tis the bridge the Mussulmen must skate over into Paradise – 'tis Al Sirach, by Jingo! Look at the depth beneath – but there's water – ah, and a ship verily, at this moment, is gliding majestically beneath!' –

'Hold your noisy tongue,' said Pedestres, checking him; "tis the Menai Bridge.'

'Horse's leg!' exclaimed the other; 'oh that ever I should have lived to behold the Menai Bridge! – Truly we have not walked 500 miles for nothing!'

At the first glance, Pedestres was disappointed; and we have already told the reader, that the same feeling attended him at Pont y Diafol. Things are vaunted so highly both by the tongues of returned volumes, that the glowing imagination is excited to create a picture that never can find a reality; so that when the picture so imagined is brought in actual comparison with the thing itself, a sensation of disappointment arises in course. As he looked at the bridge, the Holyhead mail passed over: – and then, oh then, did proportions assume their true force, and regret sprung up into wonder. The coach and horses appeared no bigger than Queen Mab's chariot, made of half an empty hazelnut, drawn with a team of little atomies; – but by weighing known certainties against fantasies of the mind, the coach soon took its real magnitude, and from this, as a scale, the dimensions of the bridge came out in forcible grandeur.

A large vessel passed under whilst Pedestres stood on the roadway; and the effect of looking down on the truck, and then the deck so far below, was strange and remarkable. The best way, however, to see the bridge to advantage is to approach by water, and look up; and in this way it is probable that the visitor may be struck with admiration at the *first* impression.

Pedestres, and Sir Clavileno:
'A Pedestrian Tour Through Wales and England' (1836)

Like Robinson Crusoe

As we crossed the bridge and were approaching the Anglesey shore we overtook a quaint, humorous old man with a tall white hat, a merry twinkle in his eye, and a huge cancer in his face. I fell into talk with him. 'Now,' he said as we left the bridge and walked into Anglesey, 'now you are like Robinson Crusoe, you are on your island. How should you like to live in that house all the year round, winter and summer?' he said pointing to a white house on a little rock island in the straits. I said I thought there might be worse places. 'They live like fighting cocks there,' winked the old man with a merry twinkle in his eye and his tall white hat nodding from side to side.' They have got a weir there and they catch all the fish.'

Francis Kilvert: Diary (1871)

The Menai Bridge

I heard him then, for I had just
   completed my design
To keep the Menai bridge from rust
   by boiling it in wine.
I thanked him much for telling me
   The way he got his wealth,
But chiefly for his wish that he
   Might drink my noble health.

Lewis Carroll: 'Alice Through the Looking Glass (1871)

27

Entering Ynys Môn

Coming to the Menai Bridge I asked the man who took the penny toll at the entrance, the way to Pentraeth Coch.

'You see that white house by the wood,' said he, pointing some distance into Anglesey; 'you must make towards it till you come to a place where there are four cross-roads and then you must take the road to the right.'

Passing over the bridge I made my way towards the house by the wood which stood on the hill till I came where the four roads met, when I turned to the right as directed.

The country through which I passed seemed tolerably well cultivated, the hedge-rows were very high, seeming to spring out of low walls. I met two or three gangs of reapers proceeding to their work with scythes in their hands.

In about half an hour I passed by a farm-house partly surrounded with walnut trees. Still the same high hedges on both sides of the road: are these hedges relics of the sacrificial groves of Mona? thought I to myself.

George Borrow: 'Wild Wales' (1862)

'The Mother of Wales'

The island of Mona is an arid and stony land, rough and unpleasant in its appearance, similar in its exterior qualities to the land of Pebidion, near St David's, but very different as to its interior value. For this island is incomparably more fertile in corn than any other part of Wales, from whence arose the British proverb, 'Mon mam Cymry, Mona mother of Wales;' and when the crops have been defective in all other parts of the country, this island, from the richness of its soil and abundant produce, has been able to supply all Wales.

Giraldus Cambrensis (c.1188):
'Itinery Through Wales' translated by Richard Colt-Hoare

'Low, Flat and Unpleasant'

Anglesey is denominated 'The Mother of Wales' by Giraldus Cambrensis, for he says, when all the other parts of the principality failed in their crops of corn, this alone, from its fertile soil and high state of cultivation, was able to supply them. This may have been the case in the twelfth century, when Gerald visited the country, and when the state of the population throughout the whole kingdom was very different from what it is at present. The interior of the island appeared to me to be very ill attended to in this respect: and in addition, much of the land lies in peat-bogs, or is full of low rocks, which cannot be cleared but by blasting, and that at enormous expense. There are, indeed some farms in the interior, but it is about the coast that the island is seen in the richest state, and particularly about that part which is opposite to Caernarfonshire. The general face of the country is low, flat and unpleasant; and although it has been represented as covered with wood in the time of the Druids, there is now scarcely any other than what is found in the plantation on the southern coast.

The princes of North Wales had their entire residence in this island, except when driven out for two centuries by the Irish and the Picts, till the close of the reign of the last prince. The palace was at Aberffraw; and I have been informed that some few fragments of the walls are still standing, forming now part of the walls of a barn.

William Bingley: from
'North Wales, Scenery, Antiquities, Customs: 1798-1801'

A Thoroughfare Between Two Kingdoms

. . . the chief support of the inhabitants arises from the intercourse of travellers between England and Ireland; for Holyhead is the great thoroughfare between both kingdoms, by reason of the shortness of the passage, it being but 20 leagues over at this place, and the conveniency of the packets which carry the mails being stationed here. There are three stout vessels of about 100 tons burthen each, contracted for by government of one Mr Thomas Blair, a merchant of Dublin, for £300 a year each, and £150 allowed for accidents. He has all the benefit arising from the conveyance of passengers to himself; the price of a bed in one of the cabins is half a guinea, walking upon deck or in the hold half a crown. One of these packets sails for Dublin with the English every Monday, Wednesday and Saturday; and returns from thence with the Irish mail on Sundays, Wednesdays and Fridays, wind and weather permitting.

'The harbour of Holyhead is found to be very convenient for the Northern trade when taken short by contrary winds; but as it is only one of the rough draughts of nature (man having never given a helping hand), it is not a good lying place for large shipping on North West winds. But if it was repaired, and warehouses built, it might be a convenient place for the Irish merchants to import their goods that pay English duty, being within seven or eight hours sailing of the coast of Ireland, and the merchants might have the conveniency of coming over in the packets to see their goods landed.'

'Topographia Britannica' (1783)

A General Appearance of Dearth

Anglesey (though it is called the granary of Wales) appeared to us as one continued picture of desolation; and for twenty miles of our road through it, we could not discover more than five or six corn fields, and the grass land so miserably poor that it starved rather than fed its hungry inhabitants. We undoubtedly did not see the country to the best advantage, because the excessive heat of the summer had parched up the ground, and occasioned a general appearance of dearth.

Beaumaris is a dirty sea-faring town; here is another of king Edward's castles; it is in tolerable preservation, but the eye is disgusted with new repairs; a fine old tower is frequently patched with modern masonry, in which the workman has barbarously shown his art, in the nice disposition of yellow bricks and mortar: added to this the inhabitants have made a bowling green within its walls. The guardian genii of venerable ruins must surely have been asleep when these impieties were committed . . .

Joseph Hucks: 'A Pedestrian Tour Through North Wales' (1795)

A Nineteenth Century American Tourist

The fact that the great American novelist Nathaniel Hawthorne visited and wrote about North Wales is not widely known. He got to know the region during his period as the American Consul in Liverpool.

July 19th, 1854 – A week ago I made a little tour in North Wales with Mr Bright. We left Birkenhead by railway for Chester at two o'clock; thence for Bangor; thence by carriage over the Menai bridge to Beaumaris. At Beaumaris, a fine old castle – quite coming up to my idea of what an old castle should be. A grey, ivy-hung exterior wall, with large round towers at intervals; within this another wall, the place of the portcullis between; and again, within the second wall the castle itself, with a spacious green court-yard in front. The outer wall is so thick that a passage runs in it all round the castle, which covers a space of three acres. This passage gives access to a chapel, still very perfect, and to various apartments in the towers, – all exceedingly dismal, and giving very unpleasant impressions of the way in which the garrison of the castle lived. The main castle is entirely roofless, but the hall and other rooms are pointed out by the guide, and the whole is tapestried with abundant ivy, so that my impression is of grey walls, with here and there a vast green curtain; a carpet of green over the floors of halls and apartments; and festoons around all the outer battlement, with an uneven and rather perilous footpath running along the top. There is a fine vista through the castle itself, and the two gateways of the two encompassing walls. The passage within the wall is very rude, both underfoot and on each side, with various ascents and descents of rough steps, – sometimes so low that your head is in danger; and dark, except where a little light comes through a loophole or window in the thickness of the wall. In front of the castle a tennis-court was fitted up, by laying a smooth pavement on the ground, and casing the walls with tin or zinc, if I recollect aright. All this was open to the sky; and when we were there, some young men of the town were playing at the game. There are but very few of these tennis-courts in England; and this old castle was a very strange place for one.

The castle is the property of Sir Richard Bulkely, whose seat is in the vicinity, and who owns a great part of the island of Anglesey, on which Beaumaris lies. The hotel where we stopped was the Bulkely Arms, and Sir Richard has a kind of feudal influence in the town.

In the morning we walked along a delightful road, bordering on the Menai Straits, to Bangor Ferry. It was really a very pleasant road, overhung by a growth of young wood, exceedingly green and fresh. English trees are green all about their stems, owing to the creeping plants that overrun them. There were some flowers in the hedges, such as we cultivate in gardens. At the ferry, there was a whitewashed cottage; a woman or two, some children, and a fisherman-like personage, walking to and fro before the door. The scenery of the strait is very beautiful and picturesque, and directly opposite to us lay Bangor, – the strait being here almost a mile across. An American ship from Boston lay in the middle of it. The ferry-boat was just putting off from the Bangor side, and, by the aid of a sail, soon neared the shore.

Nathaniel Hawthorne: 'Passages from the English Notebooks' (1870)

A Twentieth Century American Tourist

At Beaumaris I encountered a tall man in his forties, casually dressed and with an expensive camera around his neck. When we exchanged greetings I quickly realised that he was American.

'Is this your first visit to Wales?' I asked.

'Yeah,' he responded, 'and gee it's a real wonderful country. It's really beautiful, and do you know something? There are guys in the States who've never even heard of Wales, or, if they have, they maybe think its a county of England.'

'I can see that the Wales Tourist Board are going to have to work harder' I commented.

He then told me that he lived in Boston and was a television executive.

'Do you know where my paternal great grandfather came from' he exclaimed with a broad smile. 'Its no use me trying to pronounce the place,' he went on, and at this point he produced an ordinance survey map. 'Look, I'll show you on this.'

He pointed to Harlech.

'He was some kind of shepherd, I'm told. Isn't that something?'

I agreed that it was, and at the end of our chat we shook hands warmly.

'Enjoy the rest of your visit to Wales' I said.

'I sure will,' came the enthusiastic response. 'And I'll be back, make no mistake about that!'

Dewi Roberts: 'The Land of Old Renown' (1997)

The Curiosities of the Place

'19th August. At Bangor . . . Mr Roberts . . . accompanied us to Beaumaris where he sent for the Schoolmaster to show us the curiosities of the place. The Schoolmaster claimed acquaintance with Mr Johnson, and we walked together with our new friend to Baron Hill, the seat of Lord Bulkeley, a place of beautiful situation commanding the Castle, the Streights, and the mountains, an assemblage scarcely to be mended even by the imagination. We spent some time among the woods and the walks, and proceeded to a Castle of no small dignity or extent, yet much unknown to the talking World . . . The goats browzed upon the grass, the ivy added solemnity to the ruin, and the whole filled one's eyes with pleasure, and one's mind with respect for those who edified and those who inhabited so fine a fortification. The gentleman was desirous of showing Mr Johnson his School and so he did, and we rowed back to our good hospitable Mr Roberts, whose Wife gave us her best tea, and lodged us in her best beds.'

Hesta Thrale: Journals (1774)

The Desolate Church

It was a delightful summer morning, and my spirits were high as I trudged through the green lanes bounded by fields of luxuriant grass and waving corn. The appearance of the country was much like what I had seen in the eastern parts of the island, flat, or gently undulating; farmhouses, whitewashed, were thickly studded around, and along the lanes were a good many cottages, also whitewashed, but not very clean within so far as a glimpse of the interior through the open doors might enable one to judge. The greatest drawback in the landscape was the general absence of trees; the hedges were mere earthen banks, here and there planted with gorse or broom, so that in spite of the richness of the soil and the populousness of the country, there was a barrenness about its appearance which was not pleasing. I passed two or three chapels, square, new, whitewashed, and ugly; one or two churches, not whitewahsed, dilapidated, gray, and mouldy, stuck in the corners of fields and in other inaccessible places, as if they were never meant to be filled and that they were not filled was pretty evident. One was in the middle of a swamp which could be approached only by a causeway. I was curious to know how the people got to it in winter time, and especially how the corpses were ever got to the churchyard, but there was no one about from whom I might obtain information – indeed there was no house on either side for half a mile or more.

The grass in the churchyard was high and rank, and the tombstones were almost buried in it. It being by this time about mid-day and the walk having made me hungry, I thought the green churchyard might be a very pleasant spot to discuss the luncheon which I carried in my pocket, so I turned off the road, picked my way along the causeway, climbed over the stile into the churchyard intending to look in at the window. To my surprise the door was ajar, and I looked in expecting to see some 'aged man of mould' preparing for a funeral, or some other such ghastly office. But there was no one there. The place was as desolate if not quite as ruinous as the Halls of Ivor. The oak seats were slowly rotting to pieces, the font was dismantled, and had only a broken pedestal remaining. The altar had no covering of any sort to hide the nakedness of its moth-eaten wood, and the rails were all awry and loose. I thought at first that the church was entirely abandoned to the bats, but the sight of a damp, dingy, ragged surplice hanging over the reading desk showed that some attempt at a service was still made. A large dog-eared Prayer Book, and an immense black letter folio Bible, dated 1620, were on the desk near the surplice, but I could not see a book of any description on the seats around.

Were there any worshippers at all, I wondered, or was it utterly deserted? I could see that there had been a time when people took pride in this little building. Many of the oak seats were elaborately carved, and one large pew in a sort of recess had once been the squire's favoured seat. There were several monuments around; one very ancient, of pre-Reformation times, for it commenced *Orate pro anima* . . . Close to it was another interesting relic of times gone by. It was a monument to Hugh ap Owen, a Cavalier, 'who fought a good fight for his King and his country. A.D. 1646.' I mused on the changes that had come over the country, and the religious feelings of the people.

Robert Roberts: 'The Wandering Scholar' (1923)

A Mere Fishing Town

'Holyhead, so called from the mountain at the back of it, about one mile and a half distant, and a mile of perpendicular assent, is named by the Welsh Caergybi, or the Castle, or City of St Kybi. It is little more than a fishing town, rendered considerable by being the place of general passage to Ireland, few persons except the troops, and those connected with them, going by Park Gate. Here are three good inns, the Eagle and Child or the English House, the Welsh Head or Irish House, kept by the widow Arthur, and remarkably neat, and Lord Boston's Arms or the Welsh house. These houses, though by the names they seem to be appropriated to particular people, divide the business between them, especially the two first. The tide comes close up to the houses, and frequently overflows the parapet. Six packets attend in the harbour, and go every day in the week except Thursdays, and return the next day. This passage is performed at an average in about 12 hours, for which passengers pay half a guinea; the shortest passage has been six hours. All the bread used here comes from Dublin, 13 six-penny loaves to the dozen and a supply has frequently been wanting for a week in bad weather. Here is no fresh water in the village, except from rain. A bath and assembly room were erected in 1770 in hopes of alluring company from Ireland.'

'Topographia Britannica' (1782)

The Mail Boat

Railways and ships have vapours
Of the night train newspapers,
Steam gone,
Fish-clear cold faced air
Freshens my moist eyes,
Which stare,
Into the dark at the rail
For the slow shape of the Mail;
The station fills her stable,
Two ships linked by a cable,
Their bows
From the dock climbing,
Limpid green water lapping
Hibernia and Cambria,
They were never in closer,
As in Holyhead harbour
In love at the midnight hour.

Chas Parry-Jones

From Ireland to Holyhead

Roderick O'Flanagan's impressions of a visit to North Wales make entertaining and diverting reading. Here he writes of a voyage from Ireland to Holyhead.

We had not many fellow-passengers. Rapidly, in our fire-propelled vessel, we left the bold promontory of Ben-Hedir, the Hill of Howth, with the tragic little neighbour, Ireland's Eye, on our left. Our gaze lingered lovingly on the sharp peaks of Brayhead and the Golden Spears, thinking of happy bygone days spent in the lovely Vale of Shanganagh, so sweetly sung by our dear departed poet Denis Florence Mac Carthy. The day was pleasant, not too hot, and we had some entertaining fellow-voyagers, who reside in a beautiful house near Bray. Noon found us in mid-channel, far away from the Green

Isle, and fast approaching the land of leeks. Soon the rocky shores of Cambria rose in our front, and the sheltering arm of the Holyhead breakwater stretched forth to give us kindly greeting. As we approached the high promontory of Holyhead, Captain Varian came to us and pointed out the objects of interest to be seen from the deck of *The Rose*. The lighthouse on the pier, and farther off the bold cliffs called the South Stack, where thousands of sea-birds build their nests and bring up their callow broods. Here is another lighthouse on the South Stack, approached by a suspension-bridge, to be described more fully hereafter. The high hill, properly call the Mountain, forms a suitable background to the reach of tillage-land stretching from the rocky shore to the Mountain brow. Some white-walled houses, nestled in trees, stand amidst the fields; but we were so rapidly reaching our haven, there was brief time for our survey.

Before leaving Ireland, a kind friend procured us excellent lodging in Holyhead. We also, at his suggestion purchased the little 'Gossiping Guide', but on examination we found that, though no doubt very useful to tourists visiting North Wales from the English land, it was by no means so for us, making our journey from the opposite side of the country. Instead, then, of finding any account of Holyhead on opening the book, I had to turn to page 174 before I found even the brief notice given to the town, and as the book contains only 208 pages, the place we were to start from was nearer the end than the beginning. But we made our way despite of this disappointment.

On our arrival on shore, a comfortable omnibus, for the small charge of two shillings, including the driver's fee, brought us to our very excellent lodging, in Longford Terrace, kept by Mrs Williams. Holyhead is an island, but six miles from east to west, and four from north to south. It is estimated to contain about ten thousand acres, and the same number of inhabitants. The town is of great antiquity, and is supposed to owe its name, Holy-head, to the piety of the ancient population. Judging from the great number of places of worship we saw, it does not seem to have deteriorated in this respect, and, indeed, the quiet, cleanly, civil and industrious deportment of the inhabitants reflects credit upon their religious teaching, whatever creed they profess. The town is built on the slope of a steep hill washed by the waves of St George's Channel, and for centuries has been the chief Welsh port of ingress and egress to and from Ireland.

Roderick O'Flanagan: 'Through North Wales with my wife' (1884)

The View from Caer Gybi

Following the direction of the veteran Pennant, to obtain the most extensive view of the remarkable town and islet of Holyhead, I bent my way to the summit of the mountain of Caer Gybi, accompanied by the friend I had before accidentally met with in Carnarvonshire. It was that same Caer Gybi on which anciently stood the Druidical altar of sacrifice, and where afterwards arose an encampment for the conquering Roman, of which there are still sufficient fragments left to point out the figure of its enclosing wall. At every step I observed evidences of the rapid increase of this once poor fishing village, as Holyhead might formerly have been called, now spreading on every side, and supporting an active and flourishing population. From the summit we had a complete view of the promontory, and could mark its varying breadth and inequalities, and its storm-indented figure. It was approaching the hour of high water, and I could distinguish the lashing of the waves upon the precipices which tower sublimely above the ocean; and the scream of the sea-birds, sailing around the tremendous caverns open to the waters, might be distinctly heard.

Far below me lay the Pier on the island of Ynys Halen, with the Lighthouse at the extremity; the harbour with its vessels and smaller craft in different stages of preparation; and close to the quay, the Post-office packet busily preparing for immediate sail. I was struck with the singular wildness and variety of the prospect far over sea and land; the vast expanding waters – the Skerry rocks – the lighthouses, and other objects of interest, opened out on every side perspicuously to the view.

Thomas Roscoe: 'Wandering and Excursions in North Wales' (1853)

The Druids

This part of North Wales in pagan times observed the Druid rites. Druidical worship was known to have very extensively prevailed in the island of Mona in early times, but the face of the country must have greatly changed since. The name Druid is said to be from Draos, an oak, and the Druidical worship to be celebrated in oak groves; but now there is not a grove of wood of any great extent visible, except at Penrhos, near Holyhead. It is said the Romans extirpated Druidism, and it is suggested that, in order to do so effectually, they burnt the oak woods. If so, they carried out their object, for these trees are not to be seen, and the Welsh Druids are as scarce as the Welsh goats – not one goat did we see. Druid worship prevailed among Celtic nations in Ireland and in Wales, and in both countries the form of worship was doubtless much the same; but while in Ireland we still have the oak and the mistletoe, both are absent from Anglesey.

There are, however, several remains of the extinct Druidical worship around Holyhead, in the presence of cromlechs, and traces of the conquering Roman legions are pointed out. Many fine marine views can be had by ascending the elevated land called the Mountain, near the town. In the direction of the Mountain is the residence of the Panton family, a place called Garreg Lwyd (the House of Grey Stone) surrounded by trees, in which numerous noisy rooks have their nests. An ancient Church, called Capel-y-Gorlas-Angbee (the Chapel of the High Court), is adjacent. A well, Ffynnon-y-Gorlas (the Well of the High Court), is close to it. A prostrate cromlech can be seen near to these places. Tradition relates that this was the battle-field where the united warriors of North and South Wales combined, under the command of Prince Caswallan-law-her, to wrest Mona (the Isle of Anglesey) from the yoke of an Irish chief named Larigi. The Irish having resolved to make a resolute stand at Holyhead, the Welsh troops crossed the Menai straits, and gave battle. The Irish chief being slain in a hand-to-hand encounter with Caswallan, his forces were dispirited and fled to their ships, leaving the Welsh in possession of their native soil.

Roderick O'Flanagan: 'Through North Wales with my wife' (1884)

Stimulating Air

The line to Holyhead passes a cluster of lakes of not much beauty – that of Llyn Penllyn has a little island in it – then it crosses a causeway into Holy Isle, and draws up at the terminus of Holyhead, under Pen Caergybi, the highest elevation in Anglesey.

Ruskin says:-

'Just on the other side of the Mersey you have your Snowdon and your Menai Straits, and that mighty granite rock beyond the moors of Anglesey, splendid in its heathery crest, and foot planted in the deep sea, once thought of as sacred – a divine promontory, looking westward, the Holy Head or Headland, still not without awe when its red light glares first through the gloom.'

The cliff scenery here is of the finest quality, and Holyhead well merits a prolonged visit, what with the stimulating air rushing through one's lungs charged with sparkles, the look-out on the green sea flecked with foam and skimmed by gulls as flakes of froth that have been detached from the waves and become alive, the plunging water on the beach, the purple folds of the hills, and the abrupt cliffs, their feet ever bitten into and worried by the angry waves.

The town is as busy as Beaumaris is inert. It lives on the Irish trade, whereas Beaumaris picks up subsistence during a few short months only from bathers.

S. Baring Gould: 'A Book of North Wales' (1905)

A Dreadful Prospect

The town of Amlwch is about a mile from the summit of the Parys mountain and on the morning after my arrival, I walked up to this celebrated place. Having ascended to the top, I found myself standing on the verge of a vast and tremendous chasm. I stepped on one of the stages suspended over the edge and the prospect was dreadful. The number of caverns at different heights along the sides, the broken and irregular masses of rock which everywhere presented themselves, the multitudes of men at work in different parts, and apparently in the most perilous situations, the motions of the whimsies and the raising and lowering of the buckets, to draw out the ore and rubbish; the noise of picking the ore from the rock, and of hammering the wadding, when it was about to be blasted; with at intervals, the roar of the blasts in distant parts of the mine, altogether excited the most sublime ideas, intermixed, however, with sensations of terror. I left this situation and followed the road that leads to the mine; and the moment I entered my astonishment was again excited. The overhanging rocks, which seemed to threaten annihalation to anyone daring enough to approach them, fixed me almost motionless on the spot. To look up from hence, and observe the people on the stages a hundred and fifty feet above one's head; to see the immense number of ropes and buckets, most of them in motion, and to reflect that a single stone casually thrown from above might in a moment destroy a fellow creature, a man must have a strong mind not to feel impressed with many unpleasant sensasions. A few days before I left here, a bucket caught against the point of a rock, emptied its contents on the head of a poor fellow and killed him on the spot.

William Bingley: 'North Wales: Scenery, Antiquities, Customs' (1804)

39

Grand and Striking

Amlwch is a small sea port, from whence the copper (that is found in the Paris and Mona mines, which are not more than a mile from the town), is shipped to London, Liverpool, &c. The Mona mine produces the finest ore; they also make quantities of copper from old iron.

These mines have an appearance uncommonly grand and striking – a vast yawning chasm, displaying full to the view of the astonished stranger its sulphurous contents; hundreds of workmen employed in a variety of different occupations; some boring shafts, others selecting the ore, which is slung up to the top, or, if I may use such an expression, ushered into the world in little baskets. In some places the chisel and the pick-axe find room for employment; in others the men are sedulously engaged in blowing up large pieces of the rock by means of gunpowder, the report of which reverberating from side to side, in this immense cavity, occasions such a tremendous explosion, that all nature seems to tremble to its center.

Joseph Hucks: 'A Pedestrian Tour Through North Wales' (1795)

Penmon
To W.J.G.

Fine to remember our jaunt
In high spirits to Penmon.
A marvellous day it was,
Sunday surpassing Sundays;
In this journey we found peace,
Experience of pilgrims.

On Môn, the freshness of May,
On its brim, beauteous Menai's
Filigreed torque stretched like one
Tress of luminous crystal;
Flowers were thick underfoot,
We walked amidst their beauty;
We wished to recall their names
And take two of the fairest
Among them, but could not choose –
Was not each one a jewel?

From bare rock, we heard the cry
Of a gull, salt sea's daughter;
Her wings were beating briskly,
Smooth, bright, like a sword blade's stroke;
She flashed, soared in a spiral,
Turned at the height of the sky;
Sprightly she was and graceful
Lighting on the foam-white crest
Of the wave that danced beneath;
Till lovely was her leaving
Atop the billow's tossings,
Water's butterfly, wave's gem.

And the heron on the verge,
Far off, sea's mournful hermit;
He stood, the blue-grey dreamer,
On a bit of stone, the tide,
Swell's white ferment flinging spray,
Around him playing, rinsing;
He stayed without essaying
A change of look, or one turn,
Listener to the breakers' roar,
Sea miracles' mute watchman.

We reached Penmon and remained
Where summer spread wild roses
On briars like a splendid dawn,
And a blush along the thorn-twigs.

Lovely, once, was the Abbey,
We wondered how it once looked,
And, from the past, before us,
The walls now resumed their form;
Rich craft, its portal and door,
Slender its marble towers;
Haven for the weak its hall,
And holy every chamber;

The dove-cote's turret of stone
Above the berried hillside
Rose to the fair sky's airy
Elation, like sabre or sword;

And there beneath the bushes,
Heavens of leaves for its roof,
The ancient lake sleeps calmly
Below the laced branches' dusk.

At the brink was a cold spring,
And mirror-like its brightness;
As fine as a drink of wine
Its cold foam for a pilgrim.
And then there came a sweet song,
For a brief while, soft vespers;
Concord of bells and organ,
Fleeting voices pouring chant
To heaven's land, in Latin;

Though we searched the scene again,
Nothing more, except the fair
Leaves on the ruin's fragments,
And a deep benign stillness –
Of Môn's monks, we saw no more!

T. Gwynn Jones, translated by Joseph P. Clancy

An Augustinian Priory

Penmon Priory, an Augustinian house which flourished during the late
Middle Ages, was, like the foundation on Puffin Island, associated with
Seiriol. Undoubtedly he was one of the foremost saints of the island,
sharing this distinction perhaps with Cybi of Holyhead, his counterpart
in the extreme west. There is a story to the effect that these two
contemporaries used to meet each week near Llanerchymedd, in the
central north of Anglesey. There they had two wells, Cybi's and Seiriol's.
Because of the direction of their walk to and from this meeting place one
(Cybi) always had his face in sunshine, and became known as Cybi the
Dark; the other, the sun at his back, remained pale, and became known as
Seiriol the Fair. Somehow Matthew Arnold got hold of this story, but
rather absurdly understood it the wrong way round. He seems to have
assumed that the saints met at sunset, and were called dark and fair
through being, respectively, in shade and light, rather than through being
sunburnt and pale.

One came from Penmon westward, and a glow
Whiten'd his face from the sun's fronting ray;
Eastward the other, from the dying day,
And he with unsunn'd face did always go.

Seiriol the Bright, Kybi the Dark! men said.
The seer from the east was then in light,
The seer from the West was then in shade.

Arnold then goes on to make an analogy (the title of his poem being 'East and West') the deep significance of which quite escapes me.

Seiriol's priory church at Penmon, as it stands now, dates from the twelfth century onwards. (The roofs are modern, and the adjoining Priory House was restored and modernized in 1923). Among many other items of interest inside the church (a rich store of fine carved stones) is a pre-Norman cross, dated at about 1000. It bears on its sides, distinctly carved, the much-travelled and long-living ornamentation known as the Greek key pattern. A similar cross stands in a field about a quarter of a mile west-north-west of the church.

The remains of a cloister and a fine thirteenth-century refectory stand trouped around the Priory on the south side. The beautiful and sturdy dovecote nearby, with its stone vaulted roof, dates from about 1600.

Michael Senior: 'Portrait of North Wales' (1986)

No Passage Landward
(For my brother, Gareth)

A bell at Penmon warns of rocks,
their presence wrapped in bladderwrack,
looming under the channel.
On the sea horizon grey tanker
silhouettes edge on their way to or from
the oil terminal near Liverpool.

Our maternal grandparents lodged
at Penmon, down from The Pool
for Winnie to recuperate
from a miscarriage, lapsing thyroid.
The wind pressed over turfy grass,
cleaved round fossil-laden cliffs.

Since you ask, Yes, I could live here,
pass the seasons in reading the sea,
count the waves, boats passing offshore,
fish for mackerel, just sail this notched,
serrated coastline, past the lighthouse
with, painted on it, No Passage Landward.
But cars litter the headland and one
of the empty coastguard houses is for sale.
You can buy ice-lollies at the neat
Café laid in a windless fold.

I think of Winnie, that mature
woman with dark curls, hair nicking
her pale bonnet's round edge, leaning
into the perpetual breeze off
the headland, waiting for Harry's return
from the dell below, where he cut
honeysuckle with short arcs
of his penknife, eyes intent
on twisted stems, her eyes on him,
bacchic scent welling up the slope.

Behind us all is an Augustinian
priory, once a Celtic monastery,
telling the old tale, Christianity
overtaken by Rome's emissary,
the political prelate imposing
authority on earlier, subtler
visions: there our tale began.

Where are the things we imagined?
The elements still carry out
their astringent work, sharpen
over the headland traced by thousands
of lives, wiped by the wind.
The bell tolls now over a choppy sea,
boats lean, strain in the narrow strait;
There is no passage landward.

Peter Gruffydd

Plas Newydd

Begun Thursday, Aug[t] [9th], 1810. – Set off from Carnarvon. Ride charming over the Menai. Road remarkably fine and strait. Pass Llanfair is gaer, charmingly wooded down to y[e] water's edge – so called, I imagine, from its situation below a small Encampment, perhaps of the Romans, to cover their debarkation when they crossed over to Anglesey, the place nearly opposite being called Pant yr Yscraphie, or rather Pont, as it may be supposed they went over by a bridge of boats, in this place the shallowest part of the Fretum. The grounds of Plas Newydd much enlarged since the accession of those formerly belonging to Col. Peacock, and the whole enclosed with a high stone wall. We enter at a gate a little beyond Plas Coch, an old house of Queen Elizabeth's Age, and wind through very fine woods and lawns, till we come to the so much admired Druid Relic erroneously called a Cromlech.

The House is entirely new cased with most beautifully coloured grey limestone finely cut, all but polished, in the Gothick stile, as are the Offices likewise. Within, the Rooms are very magnificent, and well disposed of, particularly the Hall, in which are some fine Portraits, particularly the first Earl of Uxbridge and Lord Holland, in Charles's time. The Chapel is extremely beautiful, on the first landing place, as is the grand Staircase. The hangings of the great drawing room fronting the Menai were a present from the Queen; are India Taffeta with coloured flowers. Two of the best bed chambers are hung with silk and coloured flowers, but not so rich.

We quit the grounds by a different gate, and at every step have cause to admire the fine view of the mountains and the Menai, which here certainly presents the best appearance, as it takes a bend well calculated to show it to advantage. The Place is kept in a manner that does infinite credit to the possessor.

Richard Fenton: 'Tours in Wales: 1804–1813'

Porth Cwyfan

June, but the morning's cold, the wind
Bluffing occasional rain. I am clear
What brings me here across the stone
Spit to the island, but not what I shall find
When the dried fribbles of seaweed

Are passed, the black worked into the sandgrains
By the tide's mouthing. I can call nothing my own.

A closed-in, comfortless bay, the branchy
Shifts of voyage everywhere. On a slope
Of sand reaching up to the hidden
Field or stretch of marram a tipwhite, paunchy
Terrier sits pat on his marker, yapping me
Bodily out of range. What in God's name is he
Guarding that he thinks I want of a sudden?

To the left is the island, granite-hulled
Against froth, the chapel's roof acute
As Cwyfan put it when the finer
Passions ruled, convergent answers belled
Wetherlike towards God. Ahead is the cliff
Eaten by sand. On the quaking field beyond
Low huts, ordered and menacing. Porth China.

Once on the island those last shingle
Feet I came by seem in threat.
Can you, like Beuno, knit me back severed
Heads, Cwyfan, bond men to single
Living? Your nave has a few wild settles
And phantasmagoric dust. And Roger Parry,
Agent to Owen Bold, has a stone skew-whiff in the yard.

Doubling back again is a small
Inevitable tragedy, the umpteenth
In a sinuous month. Now I avoid
The violent pitch of the dog, with all
And nothing to guard, remark his croup,
The hysteric note in the bark. Two dunlin,
Huffing on long legs, pick in and out of the tide.

A man on the beach, a woman
And child with a red woollen cap,
Hummock and stop within earshot,
Eyeing my blundering walk. 'Can
We get to the island?', he asks, Lancashire
Accent humble, dark curls broad. And I

Am suddenly angry. But how is my tripright sounder,
Save that I know Roger Parry and he does not?

Roland Mathias

Cable Bay

Out of a cyanic sky
with brittle moon,
a setting January sun burns a hole
in the brassey wave crested horizon,
cadmium and copper tinted spume
pulverize sand and shingle,
as tide surge oozes a lather of pink foam,
which boils in the sea of torn and shredded
kelp and weed,
jaw numbed, hunched and cold, with watered eyes,
I turn the other cheek,
and think of depths haunted by the drowned,
and shrink away, as the gulls clamour.

Brian Entwistle

History, Culture and Curiosities

Parallels

Lotus like, in stubborn selfhood,
Born of eternal tiers of consciousness,
Stands Ynys Môn, north bounded by
Ferocious scouring of the Celtic Sea;
While in the south the sly quietness
Of the Menai Straits gives reflection to
Brave protective majesty of
Eryri in its panoramic range.

In rock, there since the world began,
Lie bones of Druids, who, challenging Rome,
Were slain, but rest in sacred graves;
While far famed Roman soldiers lie in mud,
Unmarked below the Menai Straits.

As Rome departed Môn became
A Christian link with Europe and the Isles.
The Age of Saints brought holiness
And wisdom held in universal awe.
Necklaces of cells and churches
Still adorn the Island, humbly linked by
Solitary walkers, Bueno,
Seiriol, Cybi, and Tysilio.

They and their successors lived to
Draw reverence from Princes, just and brave,
Who brought the law to Cymru and
Instilled respect for every living
Man and woman throughout the land.
In Ynys Môn their peaceful spirits live
Where palaces stood by the sea.

At last they rose again as the young man
Henry, from Penmynydd Tudors
Marched and fought to claim his realm at Bosworth.

The Tudors had their triumphs; the
Monarchy declined, but in Ynys Môn
The people moved, to work the land,
And painfully mine the hills of copper.
Their business thrived, and future dreams
Of workmen's pride and ownership were theirs.
The railways came; the bridge was built;
The people moved to other mainland mines.
They debated, faced the masters,
Earned at last a living family wage,
With houses, bright and warm and dry.

And still that stubborn Island soul lives on
In Ynys Môn, where farmers fight
For livelihoods and families and pride.
Still people cherish hard won power
By digging out corruption with their right
And bold insistence on the law.

As the still lotus means eternity,
So Ynys Môn, in shifts of time,
Yet signifies to Cymru and beyond
Her sustenance as 'Mam Cymru'.

Kathleen Lloyd Morris

A Centre of Resistance

Four principal tribes settled in what is now Wales: Demetae and Silures
in the south, Deceangli and Ordovices in the north, and by the time the
Romans arrived these people had become, so to speak, the Metropolitan
Celts. The religious and cultural focus of the Celtic race, subdued on the
continent of Europe by Roman power, had retreated into Wales, and
particularly into the far north-western island of Môn, 'the Isle of the
Glory of the Powerful Ones'.

This remote place thus became a centre of resistance to which Celtic
partisans might look from all over Roman-occupied Europe. In its sacred
oak groves the Celtic identity was concentrated, and the champions of a
great civilization stood at bay in the heart of their remaining territories. In
Môn lived, worked, schemed and taught the Druids, the necromantic
priests of Celticism, with their marvellous store of memorized

knowledge, their command of ritual and animist dogma, their mystic hold over the public will and their alleged altars of human sacrifice. There sang the bards, the propagandists of the culture, who could inflame the people into frenzied excesses of pride. There were the warriors with their tall crested helmets and their chased shields, woad-painted, their hair grotesquely thickened with lime-wash, attended by tall dogs, riding in chariots.

The Romans entered Wales in about the year AD 50 and fought their way with difficulty towards this Celtic Betchtesgaden: not until AD 59 did they stand at last upon the Menai Strait, the narrow stretch of water which divides Môn from the mainland of Gwynedd. We do not know exactly where they made their crossing of the strait, which is nowhere more than a mile wide, but we do know just how they felt when, arriving upon its flat green shore and looking apprehensively over the water to the island beyond, they saw the Druids, their captains and their followers lined up on the opposite bank. 'At this sight', says the historian Tacitus frankly 'our soldiers were gripped by fear.'

Jan Morris: 'The Matter of Wales' (1984)

The Roman Invasion

The fearless appearance of the Britons, and the spirit which animated their whole army, struck Ostorius with astonishment. He saw a river to be crossed, a palisade to be forced, a steep hill to be surmounted, and every post defended by a great multitude, but the Roman soldiers burned with impatience for the attack. The signal was given. The river was passed with little difficulty. The struggle at the palisade was obstinate, but at last the Britons were forced to give way and fled to the ridge of their hills. The Romans pursued eagerly. Not only the light troops, but even the legionary soldiers, forced their way to the summit of the hills after a heavy shower of darts. The Britons, having neither breastplates nor helmets, could not maintain the conflict. The legions bore down all before them. The victory was decisive. The wife and daughter of Caractacus were taken prisoners. His brother surrendered at discretion. Caractacus fled for protection to Cartismandua, Queen of the Brigantes.

Tacitus: Annals of Imperial Rome (A.D. c.55-c.117)

'The Last Flourish of the Old Religion'

Although a great deal remains of the first few thousand years of Anglesey's history, the island only enters the records of Europe in about AD 61. At that date we get a tantalizing glimpse of the last flourish of the old religion.

The Druidic religion in Europe was one of the problems which the Romans found they had to tackle. It was, it seems, the source of nationalistic inspiration which nourished resistance to their orderly, well-run Empire. Julius Caesar recorded that Druidic customs were 'thought to have originated in Britain', and that Druids from Gaul went to Britain to learn the ritual That Druidism survived strongly in Anglesey is clear from the campaigns of Suetonius Paulinus, who set out from Chester to invade it sometime between Ad 59 and 61. He crossed the Clwyd near St Asaph, the Conwy valley at Caerhun, the mountains through the pass called Bwlch-y-Ddeufaen, descended to Aber and marched along the coast. The last stronghold seemed now to be beyond the Menai Straits, and many refugees had gathered there for a final stand. 'The island of Anglesey,' Tacitus writes, 'was feeding the native resistance.'

Suetonius had with him an army of two legions, 4,000 mercenaries, other infantry, and a force of cavalry. But when they came to face the Anglesey shore they hesitated. Tacitus clearly reports an eye-witness account; his father-in-law. Agricola, was with this remote army at the time.

By the shore stood an opposing battle-line, thick with men and weapons, women running between them, like the Furies in their funeral clothes, their hair flowing, carrying torches; and Druids among them, pouring out frightful curses with their hands raised high to the heavens . . .

The unaccustomed sight for a moment intimidated the soldiers. But their commanders rallied them, and the army began to surge across. A flotilla of flat-bottomed boats had come round the coast from Chester, and with these the foot-soldiers were ferried over. The attack was launched at low-tide, and the horses swam. The Druids were slain where they stood, and their sacred oak-groves systematically cut down. Tacitus refers to these as being 'devoted to cruel superstitions . . . They deemed it a duty, indeed, to cover their altars with the blood of captives, and to consult their deities through human entrails.' His account of the Druid cult, however, can hardly be taken at face value.

By a historical chance the conquest of Anglesey was not to be carried through to its full conclusion, the garrisoning and colonization which presumably would have followed the initial pillaging and burning. As Tacitus puts it, by taking so large a force so far west Suetonius had 'exposed himself to a stab in the back.' While the felling and burning of the sacred groves was proceeding, the famous revolt of the Iceni under Boudicca was breaking out in the south. Colchester was under attack. A messenger brought the bad news all the way to Anglesey, and Suetonius and his army had to leave at once and set off back on the long march south.

Agricola perhaps felt unsatisfied at having to leave this piece of work unfinished. At any rate he marched into North Wales again, having succeeded to the generalship in about AD 77. 'He decided,' Tacitus records, 'to reduce the island of Anglesey, from the occupation of which Paulinus had been recalled by the revolt of all Britain.' This time, it seems, the inhabitants were a little better prepared. From previous experience they expected the army to be provided with a fleet, which, apparently through the haste with which the attack was conceived, they were not. Agricola picked men 'who had experience of fords and had been trained at home to swim with arms and horses under control beside them.' He was then able to launch a surprise attack, since the Welsh were still waiting for the fleet to appear in the Straits. Outwitted, they surrendered.

Michael Senior: 'Portrait of North Wales' (1986)

Roman Shackles

. . . the poor and famous Isle of Mona, never before that we hear of conquered by an enemy, was fain to put on the Roman shackles; under which it continued to groan some hundreds of years; but yet in this to be comforted, if there be any comfort in the loss of liberty, that she had her fetters put on by the two greatest Romans that ever trod on British ground; the former of them Paulinas Suetonius well deserving, and went once well nigh (if we believe Tacitus) to be chosen emperor; and the latter Julius Agricola appear'd so brave in all his actions that he was equally fear'd and envy'd by Domitian; as if his laurels had spread and mounted so high, as to begin to cast an umbrage on Caesar's diadem.

In this condition I must leave the poor island at this time, when those grand instruments of providence, the Romans, having now chas'd away her superstitious druids, and unmasked her face to her ancient shades of heathenism, had made thereby a happy undesigned way for the light of the Gospel to shine upon it, which it now began to do, and by subjugating the bodies, lives and fortunes of the Britons to Caesar's sceptre, gave them an opportunity, which was shortly after done even to the extremest corners of the land, as Tertullian assures us, of bringing their souls to the obedience of Christ.

Henry Rowlands: 'Mona Antiqa Restaurata' (1723)

Defeating the Edwardian Troops

The shore near Porth-amel is famed for being the place where Suetonius landed and put an end in this island to the Druid reign. There are no traces of any Roman works left in this country. Their stay was so short that they had no time to form any thing permanent.

About 3 miles from this place is Moel-y-Don ferry. The army of Edward I in 1282 made here an attempt fatal to many a gallant man. He landed his forces in the island and, after reducing to obedience the few inhabitants who had not taken the oath of fealty to him, built a bridge of boats near this place; some say at the very spot where Agricola passed. The Welsh, aware of his deisgn, flung up entrenchments to secure the entrance into the mountains. Luke de Tany, a commander who had lately come from Gascony with a number of Gascon and Spanish troops, rashly passed over the unfinished bridge at low water, in contempt perhaps of the enemy. The flowing tide cut off access to the nearest part of the bridge and the Welsh suddenly rushed on them with hideous shouts, slew numbers and forced the remainder into the sea. On this occasion perished Tany himself, Roger Clifford the younger, 13 knights, 17 young gentlemen and 200 soldiers. William Latimer alone escaped by the goodness of his horse which swam with him to the bridge.

Thomas Pennant: 'A Tour in Wales' (1784)

Din Lligwy which is situated near Moelfre, is a hut group dating back to the early part of the first millennium AD. It is one of the best known and most interesting pre-history sites in North Wales.

Din Llugwy

Hidden above the bay
by palisade of trees
she plays house with her doll
greets relatives at doorways.

Smoke from the smithy
spirals over thatch;
mist settling
on a field of mushrooms.

She walks on the walls,
torcs of pitted stone,
their pattern buried
in her own genes.

Women sweep children
from under a cart
to bowls of laver bread
breakers of milk.

She waves goodbye,
this child of raiders,
raised to survive
winter's icy squall.

Huw Jones
Translated by the poet

Ynys Seiriol

Just off the coast is Ynys Seriol, or Puffin Island, with the tower and ruins of a church on it. Hither retreated the monks of the first Celtic monastery to die and be buried, and the soil is dense with their bones. The rabbits turn them up when burrowing. Here, according to tradition, Maelgwn, king of Gwynedd, was buried in 547. He was son of Caswallon, who drove the Irish out of Anglesey. Maelgwyn was a remarkable man, tall and noble of countenance, and a masterful prince. He incurred the wrath of the ecclesiastics because he had once been a monk and had thrown aside the cowl. He was not particularly scrupulous about the rights of sanctuary claimed by the saints, and he was imperious in requisitioning meals of them when hunting in their neighbourhood.

He was however, large-hearted and liberal, and when Caw, a prince of Strathclyde, and his sons came helter-skelter into Gwynedd, flying from the Picts, he generously received them and gave them lands in Anglesey.

Somewhat later, Gildas the historian, one of the sons of Caw, when himself safe in Brittany, wrote his venomous letter on the *Destruction of Britain*, and thus indecently and ungratefully attacked Maelgwn, the protector of his family:-

'Thou island dragon, first in wickedness, exceeding others in power and in malice, *liberal in giving*, but more prompt in sin, strong in arms, but stronger in what destroys the soul, why dost thou wallow in such a black pool of crimes? Why dost thou lade thy neck with such loads of heavy crimes? Thy conversion once on a time brought as much joy as now thy accursed reversion to thy disgusting vomit, like a sick dog, has caused sorrow. Thy ears are not given to listen to sacred hymns, but to the bawling of a rascally crew howling out lies and frothing phlegm, be-spattering everyone round about.'

S. Baring Gould: 'A Book of North Wales' (1903)

Observing the Wildlife

About a mile farther I visited the Priory of Penmon, placed like the former on the shore. The remains are the ruinous refectory and the church; part of the last is in present use. Within is a small monument informing us that Sir Thomas Wilford of Ildington in Kent (one of whose daughters married Sir Richard Bulkeley) died January 25th 1645.

About a mile from the shore is Ynys Seiriol. The first recluses of this island, according to Giraldus, were hermits of whom (as usual) he tells a superstitious tale that they were plagued with swarms of mice whenever they disagreed. At the dissolution the revenues were valued at 47 pounds 15 shillings 3 pence, granted in the 6th of Queen Elizabeth to John More.

Ynys Seiriol is about a mile long and bounded by precipices except on the side opposite Penmon, and even there the ascent is very steep. The land slopes greatly from the summit to the edge of the precipices. During part of summer the whole swarms with birds of passage. The slope on the side is animated with puffin auks which incessantly squall round you, alight and disappear into their burrows, or come out, stand erect and gaze at you in a most grotesque manner, then take flight and either perform their evolutions about you or seek the sea in search of food. They appear first about the 5th or 10th of April but quite the place, almost to a bird, twice or thrice before they settle. Their first employ is in the forming of burrows, which falls to the share of the males who are so intent on the business as to suffer themselves at that time to be taken by the hand. Some few save themselves the trouble of forming holes and will dispossess the rabbits who, during the puffin season, retire to the other side of the island.

They lay one white egg. Males as well as females perform the office of sitting, relieving each other when they go to feed. The young are hatched in the beginning of July. The parents have the strongest affection for them but this affection ceases at the time of re-migration, about the 11th of August. They then go off, to a single bird, and leave behind the unfledged young of the later hatches as prey to the peregrine falcon which watched the mouth of the holes for their appearance, compelled as they must soon be by hunger to come out.

The food of these birds is sprats, or sea-weeds, which makes them excessively rank, yet the young are pickled and preserved by spices, and by some people much admired.

The channel between Ynys Seiriol and Ynys Môn has produced some very uncommon fish. The Biwmares shark, the morris, and the trifurcated hake are new species taken in this sea. The new mussel, called the umbilicated, is also frequently dredged up in the neighbourhood of this isle.

Thomas Pennant: 'A Tour in Wales' (1784)

Giraldus in Ynys Môn

As many things within this island are worthy of remark, I shall not think it superfluous to make mention of some of them. There is a stone here resembling a human thigh, which possesses this innate virtue, that whatever distance it may be carried, it returns, of its own accord, the following night, as has often been experienced by the inhabitants.

There is a small island, almost adjoining to Anglesey, which is inhabited by hermits, living by manual labour, and serving God. It is remarkable that when, by the influence of human passions, any discord arises among them, all their provisions are devoured and infected by a species of small mice, with which the island abounds; but when the discord ceases, they are no longer molested. Nor is it to be wondered at, if the servants of God sometimes disagree, since Jacob and Esau contended in the womb of Rebecca, and Paul and Barnabas differed; the disciples also of Jesus disputed which of them should be the greatest, for these are the temptations of human infirmity; yet virtue is often made perfect by infirmity, and faith is increased by tribulations. This island is called in Welsh, Ynys Lenach, or the ecclesiastical island, because many bodies of saints are deposited there, and no woman is suffered to enter it.

We saw in Anglesey a dog, who accidentally had lost his tail, and whose whole progeny bore the same defect. It is wonderful that nature should, as it were, conform itself in this particular to the accident of the father. We saw also a knight, named Earthbald, born in Devonshire, whose father, denying the child with which his mother was pregnant, and from motives of jealousy accusing her of inconstancy, nature alone decided the controversy by the birth of the child, who, by a miracle, exhibited on his upper lip a scar, similar to one his father bore in consequence of a wound he had received from a lance in one of his military expeditions.

In our times, also, when Henry II was leading an army into North Wales, where he had experienced the ill fortune of war in a narrow, woody pass near Coleshulle, he sent a fleet into Anglesey, and began to plunder the aforesaid church, and other sacred places. But the divine vengeance pursued him, for the inhabitants rushed upon the invaders, few against many, unarmed against armed; and having slain great numbers, and taken many prisoners, gained a most complete and bloody victory. For, as our Topography of Ireland testifies, that the Welsh and Irish are more prone to anger and revenge than any other nations, the saints, likewise, of those countries appear to be of a more vindictive nature.

Giraldus Cambrensis: 'Itinerary Through Wales'
translated by Richard Colt-Hoare (1188)

The Stone of the Thigh

I must not pass unnoticed the celebrated stone of Maen Morddwyd *(the stone of the thigh)*, now well secured in the wall of Llanidan church. In old times it was so constant to one place that, let it be carried ever so far, it would be sure of returning at night. Hugh Lupus, Earl of Chester, determined to subdue its loco-motive facilities, fastened it with iron chains to a far greater stone and flung it into the sea; but, to the astonishment of all beholders, it was found the next morning in its usual place.

Thomas Pennant: 'A Tour in Wales' (1784)

Turbulent Aberffraw

Aberffraw is a village in the south west of the island and the Princes of Gwynedd had their main court there. It was there in the thirteenth century that Llywelyn ap Iorwerth attempted to re-unite the Welsh nation, which had been in a state of rivalry and conflict.

In 966, Aberffraw, the royal seat of the Princes of North Wales, was destroyed by the Irishmen, 'when Rodri the son of Idwal, was slain in Aberffraw.' The union, so long subsisting between the Princes of North Wales, Ieva and Iago, was at this period fatally dissolved by force of arms. Iago seized the person of his brother Ievaf, and consigned him to a tedious imprisonment. In 968, Howel, son to the captive prince, raised an army to deliver his father out of prison. It was an evil peculiarly fatal to the independency of Wales, (and produced by its civil dissentions) that the weaker party usually fled for protection to the Kings of England. We learn from the Black Book of Basingwerk, that Howel was accompanied by a strong body of English, who over-ran and destroyed Llŷn and Mona, taking possession of the lands of Iago, from which they were never fairly extirpated, and this was the occasion of calling the Island of Môn, Anglesey, that is, the Island of the English.

We have room to infer that Aberffraw was a favourite residence with Llewelyn and his Princess Joan of England, who was, agreeable to her desire, buried upon the sea-shore at Llanvaes; the prince building over her remains a house of barefoot friars. In 1237, early in the spring, and soon after the death of his princess, Llewelyn's character, which had hitherto appeared with so bright a lustre, shewed symptoms of declining vigour. In a moment of weakness, and perhaps the desire of repose, he put himself under the protection of Henry III. King of England, naming his youngest son David, (nephew to that ambitious monarch) heir to the principality, when Gryffydd, his son by a fomer marriage, was still alive, possessing many qualitites, which, among a people like the Britons, were held in high estimation, and very brave in war,' tall and comely in person, &c. and being the eldest son of Llewelyn, was heir apparent to the crown. Taking advantage of his father's infirmities, David entered his brother Gryffydd's territories, seized him when in company with the Bishop of Bangor, and confined him in the castle of Criccieth, a fortress situated on the verge of the sea, in Caernarvonshire. The treatment of this popular prince excited the greatest emotion, and North Wales, for some time was deluged in blood, of the 'beste of her people'. In this state of affairs died Llewelyn, after a prosperous reign of fifty-six years. His talents and virtues, with the fortunate direction of both, have given this prince the illustrious title of 'Llewelyn the Great'.

Angharad Llwyd: 'A History of the Island of Mona' (1833)

At the Palace Gates

The holding of the *Porthorion* or gatekeepers at the Porter's Lodge was probably a survival from before the conquest. Though no prince now lived at the Palace of Aberffraw, its walls were not at once allowed to decay. It continued as a Court and a prison if not as a palace. The porter *(porthaur)* under the Venedotian Code was an important official. He had his dwelling in the gateway, and had charge of the great gate, and in his house lodged the King's and the Queen's 'door-wards'. He was to summon the men of the *Maerdref* to work. His land and the land of the door-wards were free by reason of their office, and having the responsibility of the gate it was natural (though not stated in the Code) that the responsibility of keeping the wall on both sides of the gate in repair should rest upon the gatekeepers and be attached to their land.

The smiths and the carpenters may also well be survivals. According to the Venedotian Code, the smith of the Court had to do all needful work for the palace (except certain things) and had his land free on account of his office. His work could hardly be dispensed with, whether the shoeing of horses or the mending of the ploughs of the *Maerdref,* or of the hinges of the gates, or the fastening or unfastening of the prisoners' chains, all of which were items of his duty under the Codes.

There is a small fragment of the Court Roll of Aberffraw, dated 1346, at the Record Office, which shows that the porters still had charge of the prison, for it contains an entry of a fine one the porters received for allowing prisoners to escape.

Frederick Seerbohm: 'The Tribe System in Wales' (1895)

The Triumphs of Owen

Owen's praise demands my song,
Owen swift, and Owen strong,
Fairest flower of Roderic's stem,
Gwynedd's shield, and Britain's gem.
He nor heaps his brooded stores,
Nor on all profusely pours;
Lord of every regal art,
Liberal hand and open heart.
Big with hosts of mighty name,
Squadrons three against him came;
This the force of Eirin hiding,
Side by side as proudly riding,
On her shadow long and gay
Lochlin ploughs the watery way;
There the Norman sails afar
Catch the winds and join the war:
Black and huge along they sweep,
Burdens of the angry deep.

Dauntless on his native sands
The Dragon-son of Mona stands;
In glitt'ring arms and glory drest,
High he rears his ruby crest.
There the thund'ring strokes begin,
There the press, and there the din;
Talymalfra's rocky shore
Echoing to the battle's roar.
Check'd by the torrent tide of blood
Backward Menai rolls his flood;
While, heap'd his master's feet around,
Prostrate warriors gnaw the ground.
Where his glowing eye-balls turn,
Thousand banners round him burn.
Where he points his purple spear,
Hasty, hasty rout is there,
Marking with indignant eye
Fear to stop, and shame to fly.
There confusion, terror's child,
Conflict fierce, and ruin wild,

Agony, that pants for breath,
Despair and honourable death.

Gwalchmai (circa 1130-1180)
translated by Thomas Gray

Dwynwen

William Williams gave this account of the well of St Dwynwen, the Welsh patron saint of love. It is situated on Llanddwyn Island a mile or so from Newborough.

Dwynwen was a princess in the 5th century. She fell in love with a man whom she was unable to marry because her father wished her to become the wife of another. She fervently prayed to be released from the complications of love and took up refuge in a hermitage. Before her death she expressed the wish to be allowed to watch the sunset from a particular spot on the island. It has since then been a place of pilgrimage.

There was a spring of clear water now choked up by the sand, at which an old woman from Newborough always attended, and prognosticated the lovers' success from the movements of some small eels which waved out of the sides of the well, on spreading the lover's handkerchief on the surface of the water. I remember an old woman saying that when she was a girl, she consulted the woman at this well about her destiny with respect to her husband; on spreading her handkerchief, out popped an eel from the north side of the well, and soon after another crawled from the south side, and they both met on the bottom of the well; then the woman told her that her husband would be a stranger from the southern part of Caernarfonshire. Soon after, it happened that three brothers came from that part and settled in the neighbourhood . . . one of whom . . . in a little time, married her. So much of the prophecy I remember. This couple was my father and mother.

William Williams c.1800

Affairs of Love

There was, in Dafydd ap Gwilim's time,' about the middle of the fourteenth century, 'a vast concourse from all parts of Wales to the monastery of St Dwynwen in Anglesey, now called Llanddwyn, in ruins.

Here were constant wax lights kept at the tomb of this virgin saint, where *all persons in* LOVE applied for remedy, and which brought vast profit to the monks; and Dwynwen was as famous among the Britons in affairs of love, as Venus ever was among the Greeks and Romans. But Dafydd ap Gwilim's ludicrous manner of applying to this saint for relief, and his publishing it in a poem (which is in every body's hands), shews how slightly the poet made of these religious cheats. Dear Dwynwen (says he), I, by your virginity, I beg of you, and by the soul of your great father Brychan, send this girl to meet me in the grove. You are in heaven, God will not be angry with you, nor turn you out, for he will not undo what he has done.

Lewis Morris quoted in Peter Roberts: 'Popular Antiquities of Wales' (1815)

A Sandy Coastline

I soon reached Newborough (or more properly Rhosfair, the Welsh name) about 3 miles from the shore. Here had been one of the residences of our princes. In Mr Rowlands' time, the foundation of the Llys, or palace, was to be seen a little to the south of the church. Newborough now subsists by a manufacture of mats and rhofir morhesg ropes, made of sea reed-grass. Queen Elizabeth widely prohibited the extirpation of this plant to prevent having half the parish buried in the unstable sands by the rage of the tempests. Such is the case with Llanddwyn; almost the whole is at present covered with sand-hills. In the reign of Henry VIII it was one of the richest prebends in the cathedral of Bangor. Its wealth arose not from the real fertility of the place but from the superstition of the common people; from pilgrimages to crosses, relics, holy wells, ordeals and divination from fishes.

On the peninsular are the ruins of the church, dedicated to St Dwynwen, daughter of Brychan, one of the holy Colidei or primitive Christians of Britain.

Thomas Pennant: 'Tours in Wales' (1784)

A Prayer to St Dwynwen

Dwynwen, your beauty like the hoar-frost's tears:
from your chancel with its blazing waxen candles
well does your golden image know
how to assuage the griefs of wretched men.
What man soever would keep vigil in your choir
(a holy, shining pilgrimage), you with Indeg's radiance,
there is no sickness nor heart's sorrow
which he would carry with him thence from Llanddwyn.

Your holy parish is your straggling flock:
(a man) sorrowful and worn with care I am;
because of longing for my mistress
my heart is swollen up with love,
deep pangs grounded in anxiety,
as I well know – this is my malady –
unless I can win Morfudd
if I remain alive, it is but life in vain.
Make me be healed, (you) most deserving of all praise,
from my infirmity and feebleness.
For one year be both messenger of love
as well as mediatrix of God's grace to man.
There is no need for you, unfailing golden image,
to be afraid of sin, the body's ever-present snare.
God does not undo what he has once done,
good is his peaceful disposition, you will not fall from Heaven.
No coquette will observe you now this year
whispering with us in a narrow corner.
No angry Jealous One, cruel-minded,
will put a cudgel to (your back), chaste-minded one.

Come, of your kindness (?) – quiet, you will not be suspected,
Virgin of enduring sympathy,
from Llanddwyn, a place of great resort,
to Cwm-y-gro, (you) gem of Christendom.
God has not withheld from you (easy to be reconciled),
the gift of ample speech, nor will man reject you.
Unquestionably to the work of prayer
God calls you (black your wimple).
May God, your host, restrain

the two hands of that man – may there be recalled
the violence of the person who would ravish her
when she would follow me through the leaves of May.
Dwynwen, if you would once cause
under May's trees, and in long summer days
her poet's reward – fair one, you would be good,
for, Dwynwen, you were never base.
Prove, by your gifts of splendid grace
that you are no prim virgin, prudent Dwynwen.

Because of the penance that you did
through goodness, for the world, and its significance,
because of the devotions that you kept,
while you were alive, the faith of (all those) of religious kind,
because of the true dedication of a nun,
and the virginity of the fair captive flesh
for the soul's sake – if it be needful now –
of Brychan with the powerful strong arms –
implore, by the agony caused by your faith,
of the sweet Virgin to deliver me.

Dafydd ap Gwilym
translated by Rachel Bromwich from 'Dafydd ap Gwilym: Poems' (1982)

Tony Conran has made a notable contribution to the literature of Wales as a translator, a poet and a very fine literary critic. This poem appears here for the first time.

Winter at Llanddwyn

The ruined shrine of Dwynwen
   patron saint of lovers

     Cantref of Rhosyr

Not to dance. To sit it out
In the storm, in the level sunlight
All winter, deciduous.

With wings pegged on the line
Cormorants hang like scarecrows.
The islands are so near.

The gulls' clattering quarrel
Reaches downwind
In a high melancholy wail.

It empties the air,
This winter calm.
There's nothing to think.

Will the prelude
Break on a downbeat,
A crescendo of excitement?

The curtain of time
Stays shut, curls
Only at the edge, like ripples.

Will the cold islands
Reveal themselves
A scena, or pas de deux?

* * *

A girl here. A man. An expectation.
It was as if in the gentle savagery of love
They danced, hardly touching –

Even a kiss broke the concentration
Of their waiting, even a reaching hand
Startled in a rush of wings.

In the rhyme of bodies, alliterations
Of moving together, mirrorings –
An inseparable separation.

Time was created in the first moments
When their eyes met. Like a dance
In its performance, nothing

Before that counted. Prehistory
Only inferred in the quality
Of gesture, a fossil acquaintance.

65

* * *

But then, she broke it.

– Why?

– There are answers, of course.
Father opposed to it, a dynasty
To be thought of . . . Or was it
A sudden, inexplicable
Failure of belief, an injury
Like a finger cut off
To a fiddler?

– Or did he overreach himself
In some way, and offend her?

– She showed no anger.

– He did, though.

– She had betrayed him?

– Betrayed the two of them. He saw her
Choose to make nothingness
Of what they'd been.
Very well, his body would show her –
Tell her how nothingness felt. He forced her,
Pulled her down, stripped her . . .

– Didn't she cry out?

– He left her, in the contempt he felt for her
A day and a night. She was unclean –
Her father tried to hide her
But there was nowhere left,
Nowhere beyond the mirroring.

– It was terrible for her.

– But he was destroyed by it,
Maddened by the ice
That scooped life out of him.
He would have starved . . .

* * *

It was then God chose her,
Then, or at the beginning
Of the world, in the nothingness.

It is said that an Angel came
With a new mirroring. He showed her
Maelon, her lover, frozen in the ice.

God gave her three wishes . . .

* * *

This winter calm
Empties the air.
There's nothing to think.

Though in the pool
Configurations of fishes
Prophesy (or lovers say they do)

And birds on the islands
Live out their natural
Appetitive hysterias –

The clipped sarcasm of gulls,
The cormorants –
Seals roll on their backs and sing . . .

Yet God chooses
In the nothingness
Before the curtain's drawn

Where the dancers from the green room
Wait to cross into time
As their eyes meet his

And there's nothing to think
But the dance
And the empty light.

Tony Conran

Note by the poet:
For the story of Dwynwen and Maelon see Chwedlau Gwerin Cymru/Welsh Folk
Tales *by Robin Gwyndaf (National Museum of Wales, 1992), p.37. Dwynwen's three*
wishes were first that Maelon be unfrozen; second that God would answer her
intercessions on behalf of true lovers; and third that she should never again wish to be
married.

Ffynnon Gwenfaen

Below is an extract from an article by Edward Owen which appeared in the
periodical Wales *in 1894. The author records a walking holiday with Professor*
John Rhys around the Holyhead area.

A tiring walk, but one that should by no means be omitted, is that to
Rhoscolyn Head, where the prospect of the western coast of Anglesey,
with the grand Snowdonian range in full view, is magnificent in the
extreme. Almost at the edge of the stupendous cliffs is situated the holy
well of St Gwenvaen, the patron saint of the neighbouring Church. This
well is one of those divinatory or sacred wells, to which votive offerings
were paid for the intercessory or remedial assistance of the saint. But I
could find no local tradition respecting St Gwenvaen's well to hand to
Professor Rhys, and the place is so far removed from the track of the
madding crowd that it has escaped the notice of the zealous antiquaries
of a bye-gone age. I have, however, been so fortunate as to meet with a
highly intersting reference to St Gwenvaen's Well in the manuscripts of
Lewis Morris, the antiquary, who . . . married a wife from the
neighbouring farm of Ty Wridin.

It appears that a reverend, but anonymous friend of the antiquary,
who was once vicar, – or curate, it is not clear which, – of Rhoscolyn had
removed to Beaumaris, taking with him a book entitled 'Y Rhybbudiwr
Cristionogawl', no doubt because he found it of great use in making up
'tithe sermons and other polhetick speechs'. Lewis Morris in requesting

its return, observes that the grief occasioned by the departure of his clerical friend was so general in the parish that a cave 'hight odyn gwyr Roscolun', the kiln of the men of Rhoscolyn, 'mimick'd Etna', and in order to couch his request in sufficiently persuasive terms he invokes the aid of St Gwenvaen, in these lines:-

Gwenvaen, thou chiefest in the choir of saints,
Great benefactress of Rhoscolun cell,
Thou, whilst on earth vast wonders has performed,
But now thy power no doubt is vastly great,
For even inanimate things obey thy will,
Of which the well which bears thy sacred name
Is evidence sufficient.
    Full oft have I repaired to drink that spring,
Waters which cure diseases of the soul
As well the body! and which always prove
The only remedy for want of sense.
Two white spar stones is all thou dost expect
As a free offering both for sense and health.
[What duller creature than thy present priest
Before he'd tasted of thy crystal fluid
Which presently to's blood and sleeping sense
Gave circulation, great and rare effects!
And now he lords it o'er his duller brethren
Like a game cock who's master of the field,
Strutting along, and crowing as he struts,
Wondering t'other chickens are so dull.]
'Tis thou, and thou alone, that I invoke
To lead my pen. Then grant me that small boon,
That wit and gentle sense may flow in every line
In such proportion as I've drunk thy waters.
Then distant nations shall adore thy name,
And the Crim Tartar sing thy endless fame.
'Tis done! she answers by ye bubbling spring,
Which smiles as if well pleased with my petition.
Rise, goddess, rise, and spread thy sparkling beams
Of light upon the humblest of thy servants.

Now, whether we consider that these mock-heroic lines bear evidence that the goddess heard her votary's prayer, or whether she remained obdurate, the little poem is valuable as affording possibly the only evidence in existence for the peculiar attributes of St Gwenvaen's Well.

The waters seem to have been used as a charm against mental disorders, or, as the poem implies, weak minds. We are unfortunately not told whether a certain form of incantation was used to exorcise the sluggish humours of the brain, or whether drinking of the waters conferred the power of divining the future, or merely increased intellectual capacity. Two small white pebbles constituted the propitiatory offering, which may have somehow arisen from the goddess's name, Gwenvaen or White Stone. The well is an interesting structure, and is happily in much better condition than the majority of the springs around which so much of our folklore has clustered. The well, which itself is under cover, has in front of it a small paved forecourt, the walls of which are standing to the height of about four feet. At the two corners furthest from the water, a triangular slab has been built into the walls, forming two seats, upon which no doubt, the suppliant sat to await the stirrings of the divine afflatus. Two or three steps lead down to the enclosed space before the well. The water escapes into a small trough placed outside the external wall, and thence trickles down to the edge of the cliff, over which it speeds to join the mighty ocean.

Edward Owen from 'The Antiquities of Holyhead and District' (1894)

Manikin

someone has left a manikin
on the charred ledge
it must signify something
its limbs have been bound around
meticulously
with bands of coloured wool
it is surmounted with a magpie's feather

it is a pagan thing

strange to find it here
at Saint Seiriol's well
where water bubbles softly in its square
edged by worn flags
a seat of cracked slate set in stone.

the wall is stained with damp
thrown coins squint among pebbles
the water tastes sharp, tastes cold
thinly a robin stakes his claim
on a bare elder

you keep coming back
for something you always find
but cannot name
it lives here somewhere
in the old stones, the ivy
the large leafed cresses

you hold the manikin
you twist it in your hand
some sainted hermit
stands within your light
some woman's tears are binding
the bright ply
on the peeled stick

you do not want to leave
you lift tired hands
in thin sun
setting him reverently back
lifting the latch
on a green shape

Glenda Beagan

A Sinful Nation

February 17th, 1758: This day being appointed by authority for public fast
to implore God's mercies to this sinful nation, which is roughly corrupted
by every branch of business and overwhealmed in vices of all sorts at a
time of a dangerous war that threatens a total destruction to our religion
and liberties as a free nation, yet such is the general corruption that
nothing but venality is to be found in all orders of men, divines, Courts of
Justice, the Army and Navy in so much that we are become the contempt
and derision of the world.

William Bulkeley: 'The Diary of William Bulkeley of Brynddu'
included in the Anglesey Antiquarian Transactions

Pursuing Justice

A Scotsman being drowned on Lavan Sands last winter, by the
ferrymen's refusing or neglecting to go for him, two of the said ferrymen
on the morrow went in quest of the Corpse, tore out his pockets, stole his
money, and afterwards finding his Box and Pack, carried them also away
and hid them in the Point under gravel and tang, which some of the
Town's people observing, four of them 2 sailors and 2 shipwrights went
there in the night, took them up and shared them amongst them and two
or 3 more of the contederacy. The Town Magistrates and the
neighbouring Country Justices having either neglected or refused to take
proper examinations, and to secure the Criminals, the Judges of the
Circuit (Viz) Mr Taylor Whyte and the booby Rogers Holland sent for Mr
Lewis and myself and press'd it upon us that we should take the
Examinations of such people as should be brought to us by the Solicitor of
the prosecutor, all the Criminals were of the Borough of Beaumaris; and

the Constables of the Borough took them and brought them before us, which took up all our time for the most part of 3 days.

William Bulkeley: 'The Diary of William Bulkeley of Brynddu' included in the Anglesey Antiquarian Society Transactions

Mobbing

February 8th, 1758: Mobbing has been so frequent this winter in this country and several ship loads of corn, butter and cheese have been publicly stolen and carried away, and the greater part of it never sold at all and what was sold was next to nothing.

The new Justices have adjourned the Quarter to the Shire Hall, Beaumaris, where all the farmers that have sold any corn, and those that bought it, have been summoned to attend at the peril of their lives from a mob of 200 to 300, who fill the hall and insult and abuse those already there upon their summons, who are kept there to answer the same questions asked over and over again by those threatening inquisition, who from the bench bully them, while the rude mob behind insult and abuse them, when they at last are tired and confounded and confess on themselves and are accordingly convicted and unmercifully fined.

William Bulkeley: 'The Diary of William Bulkeley of Brynddu' included in The Anglesey Antiquarian Society Transactions

Cattle Crossing

They (the cattle) are urged in a body by loud shouts and blows into the water, and as they swim well and fast, usually make their way for the opposite shore; the whole troop proceeds regularly till it arrives at about 150 yards from the landing-place, where meeting with a very rapid current formed by the tide, the herd is thrown into the utmost confusion. Some of the boldest and strongest push directly across, the more timorous immediately turn round and endeavour to return, but the greater part, borne down by the stream, frequently float to a great distance before they are able to reach the Carnarvonshire shore. To prevent accidents a number of boats well-manned attend who row after the stragglers to force them to join the main body; and if they are very obstinate, the boatmen throw ropes round their horns and fairly tow them to the shore, which resounds with the loud bellowings of those who are landed. Notwithstanding the great number of cattle that annually pass the Strait, an instance seldom, if ever, occurs of any being lost.

William Bingley: 'North Wales: Scenery, Antiquities, Customs' (1804)

Before The Revival

With reference to the first part of your letter (viz, 'What was the condition of Anglesey with regard to religion, godliness, and morality before the recent Methodist revival broke out in it?) it is not hard to answer; the common people (except one in a thousand) had no more knowledge than the wild creatures of the Mountains; they delighted in nothing except empty sport and carnal pleasures, playing with dice and cards, dancing and singing with the harp, playing football, tennis, mock-trials, and hostages, and many other sinful sports too numerous to be mentioned. – They used the Sunday like a market-day to gratify every wicked whim and passion; old and young, with no one to persuade or prevent them in their ungodly course. – They flocked in crowds to the parish churches on Sunday morning; not to listen to the word of God, but to devise and relate foolish anecdotes, and to entice each other to drink at the wash-brew house of the devil's market; and to arrange places of meeting to decide upon the sports to be engaged in after the evening service. The lads and young men, by the hundreds, kicking the Football in their pants and shirts, and belabouring each other more like dogs fighting for a bone than men bearing the name of Christians. The old men acting as spectators, encouraging and urging on – every man his party; sticks in hand, they shouted and swore in a manner which made them look more hideous than hounds. The women, in scores, contended and yelled at the top of their voices; and in their excitement and wild rage they would cast off their shawls, their hats and caps, more formidable in aspect than hags; they would run to and fro amid the crowd, shouting encouragement to relative or friend, until the field of sport became more like a battle-field of enemies, than a game between neighbours and relatives. When the game was over (if game it can be called) most of the players would be very badly hurt.

No wonder the Angleseyites were once called *Swine*; it is a wonder they were not called *Bears*, or *Lions*. Within the last sixty years, there has been many an entire parish in Anglesey, where not a single inhabitant could read one letter in a book; and not one in a thousand who saw the

74

least necessity for such an accomplishment. This was the state and condition of Anglesey when my father came first to live in it.

From a letter from Siôn Williams to the Rev. Thomas Charles c.1799
from D.E. Jenkins: 'Thomas Charles of Bala' (1908)

Ghosts and Apparitions

Ghosts and apparitions have always been very numerous in Anglesey. Many have disappeared, leaving only names in different localities, and in some cases hazy traditions to commemorate them, e.g., Craig yr Ellyll (The Goblin's Rock) in Llanddona, Lon-y-bwbach (the Bogey's lane) in Llanddyfnan, Cadair-y-bwgan (the Bogey's chair) in Llaneugrad, and some few others. With regards to the bogey's chair it has been contended that the proper name is Gwgan's chair. Gwgan was a man's name, and close by there is a farm house of the name of Cadwgan. Very little is known about this man; but the 'bwgan' of folklore was a terrible phantom, or ghost, or apparition, and used to visit the farm houses of the neighbourhood, always with some malevolent purpose, such as befouling the dairies, causing the cows to with-hold their milk, overturning the milkpails, and even bringing the animals under baleful influences. After becoming tired of tormenting the farmers and others, he would retire to his chair on the roadside to the great terror of the passers by.

Another ghost was the 'White Lady of Henllys Fawr', identical perhaps with the 'White Lady of the Gate' in the same neighbourhood. This lady-ghost was not in any sense malevolent: quite the reverse, she seemed to be actuated by a desire to disclose hidden treasures, after attaining which purpose she would not appear any more. In another part of the Island there was a lady-ghost of a different character. This ghost's habit was to walk at twilight in the garden of a certain farm house, and that in a very majestic manner. One night, one of the farm hands, a boastful fellow, declared that he would meet her on her usual walk on a certain path and would see which of them should give way to the other. The ghost appeared on the path walking slowly, and the man did the same; but when he was in close proximity to her she grinned at him and appeared to assume a menacing attitude, with the result that the man fell down in a swoon. He could not be persuaded to visit that garden at twilight any more.

W. Pritchard
in the Anglesey Antiquarian Society Transactions (1914)

The Llanddona Witches

There is a tradition in the parish of Llanddona, Anglesey, that these witches, with their husbands, had been expelled from their native country, wherever that was, for practising witchcraft. They were sent adrift, it is said, in a boat, without rudder or oars, and left in this state to the mercy of the wind and the wave. When they were first discovered approaching the Anglesey shore, the Welsh tried to drive them back into the sea, and even after they had landed they were confined to the beach. The strangers, dead almost from thirst and hunger, commanded a spring of pure water to burst forth on the sands. This well remains to our days. This miracle decided their fate. The strangers were allowed, consequently, to land but as they still practised their evil arts the parish became associated with their name, and hence the *Witches of Llanddona* was a term generally applied to the female portion of that parish, though in reality it belonged to one family only within its boundaries.

The men lived by smuggling and the women by begging and cursing. It was impossible to overcome these daring smugglers, for in their neckerchief was a fly, which, the moment the knot of their cravats was undone, flew right at the eye of their opponents and blinded them, but before this last remedy was resorted to the men fought like lions, and only when their strength failed them did they release their familiar spirit, the fly, to strike with blindness the defenders of the law.

The above-mentioned tradition of the coming of these witches to Anglesey is still current in the parish of Llanddona, which is situated on the north coast of Anglesey.

It was thought that the witching power belonged to families, and descended from mothers to daughters. This was supposed to be the case with the witches of Llanddona. This family obtained a bad report throughout the island. The women, with dishevelled hair and bared breasts, visited farm houses and requested charity, more as a right than a favour, and no one dared refuse them. *Llanddona Witches* is a name that is not likely soon to die. Taking advantage of the credulity of the people they cursed those whom they disliked, and many were the endeavours to counteract their maledictions. The following is one of their curses, uttered at *Y Ffynnon Oer*, a well in the parish of Llanddona, upon a man who had offended one of these witches:

'May he wander for ages many;
And at every step, a stile;
At every stile, a fall;

At every fall, a broken bone;
Not the largest, nor the least bone,
But the chief neck bone, every time.'

Elias Owen: 'Welsh Folklore' (1887)

Strange Howlings

According to Folklore it would appear that there were among ghosts not only different characters but different grades as well. Some of them seemed rather shy, and were content with making their presence known – nothing more; while others lurked in crossways and dark corners, as if they were of too low a degree to act otherwise. These were, apparently, the lower class, the plebeians of the ghostly community. Others were of a bolder nature, and asserted themselves by their voices, their appearances, and other signs becoming to their power and dignity. There were at least three ghosts of this class in Anglesey. One used to rove in the neighbourhood of Llanallgo and Llaneugrad; he was known as Bwgan y Parciau (the Parciau Ghost), and was commonly called the Ghost of Sir John Bodvel, because that gentleman lived in the place some three centuries ago. There is no doubt, I believe, that in the days of our fore-fathers strange howlings in the air were heard; and, to all appearance, they moved from place to place in the neighbourhood with great rapidity, as if there were two or three or more responding to each other. It is true that some people try to explain away these strange noises by saying that they were caused by foxes towards the end of their career in Anglesey. Folklore, however, would have none of such incredulous and impious opinions. There is no evidence that this ghost ever harmed anyone beyond disturbing the minds of the timid and superstitious. No such strange noises are to be heard in the neighbourhood now; and those who pretend to know the secret declare that the ghost has been deported for a certain period, to the Red Sea. At one time this ghost occupied a very conspicuous place in the Folklore not only of the district, but also of the whole Island.

W. Pritchard
in the Anglesey Antiquarian Society Transactions (1914)

The Tale of Modryb Sian

I have often heard my father relating a story about one Modryb Sian of Llanerchymedd. This Modryb Sian in her younger days was engaged as a servant at Clwchdernog. Before going there all her friends and acquaintances endeavoured to persuade her not to go and to send the earnest back as was the custom, and thereby cancel the agreement. But she was not a timid character, and she went there without fear of ghosts or anything else, and began her work in the best of spirits. While lying in bed one night she heard some strange noise in the bedroom. Afterwards came a noise as of the rending of a garment. But she did not mind it at all, and said, 'Rend a yard for me.' As soon as this was said a great noise of rending was heard above, around, and everywhere, and lasted for the greater part of the night. At last her courage gave way, and she decided to depart in the morning from such an uncanny place. As soon as she reached Llanerchymedd, and settled there, she took every opportunity to make known the ghostly experience with the result that her story appealed to the imagination and the fears not only of almost all in the township but also in every part of Anglesey.

W. Pritchard
in the Anglesey Antiquarian Society Transactions (1914)

The Tale of a Pig

A woman sold a pig at Beaumaris to a man called Dick y Green; she could not that day sell any more, but the following market day she went again to Beaumaris. Dick was there awaiting her appearance, and he told her that the pig he bought was bewitched and she must come with him to undo the curse. Away the woman went with Dick, and when they came to the pig she said, 'What am I to do now, Dick? Draw thy hand seven times down his back' said Dick, and say every time, 'Rhad Duw arnat ti,' i.e., 'The blessing of God on thee.' The woman did so, and then Dick went for physic for the pig, which recovered.

Elias Owen: 'Welsh Folklore' (1887)

The Guardian of the Treasures

There is a farmhouse called Clwchdyrnog in the parish of Llanddeusant which was said to have been haunted by a Spirit. It seems that no one would summon courage to speak to it, though it was seen by several parties. One night, however, John Hughes, Bodedern, a widower who visited the house for the purpose of obtaining a second Mrs Hughes from among the servant girls there, spoke to the ghost. The presence of the spirit was indicated by a great noise in the room where Hughes and the girl were. In great fright Hughes invoked the spirit and asked why he troubled the house 'Have I done any wrong to you?' said he, addressing the spirit. 'No,' was the answer. Then he asked if the girl to whom he was paying his respects was the cause of the spirit's visits, and again he received the answer 'No.' Then Hughes named individually all the inmates of the house in succession, and was answered in the negative. Then he asked why, since no one in the house had disturbed the spirit, he came there to disturb the inmates. To this pertinent question the spirit answered as follows: 'There are treasures on the south side of Ffynon Wen, which belong and are to be given to the nine months old child in this house; when this is done I will never disturb this house any more.' The spot occupied by the treasure was minutely described by the spirit, and Hughes promised to go to the place indicated. The next day he went to the spot, and digging into the ground, he came upon an iron chest filled with gold, silver, and other valuables; and all these things he faithfully delivered up to the parents of the child, to be kept by them for him until he should come of age to take possession of them himself. This they faithfully did, and the spirit never again came to the house.

Elias Owen: 'Welsh Folklore' (1887)

The Paradwys Ghosts

The next I shall mention is the Paradwys Ghost, – or rather Ghosts, for there were many of them. At times a voice was heard in some part of the house, and the garden, as of a child crying in great distress; and it would suddenly cease. At other times would be heard a clattering of horses' hoofs, and the rumbling of a carriage driven in hot haste towards the house. If the inmates deemed it worth their while to go out to try and see these nightly visitors, they would always be disappointed; nothing at all could be seen, nor any sign or trace of them. But on the public road, a short way above the house, this phantom turnout was occasionally seen by pedestrians who chanced to be on the road: – a gorgeous coach, two black horses panting for breath as if they had travelled from a far off region, two coach drivers sitting on high seats, cracking their whips, a stately footman at the back, and within the carriage sat a mysterious being that nobody ever knew who or what he was. At times, too, there would be a nightly hunt, horses with riders being seen following a pack of hounds, supposed to be hell-dogs (cwn annwn); and now and then was heard a turmoil of war in the woods close by. This company of ghosts seems to cling tenaciously to their rights and privileges in the neighbourhood, as there are persons living who declare that they have been eye-witnesses of some of their doings.

W. Pritchard
in the Anglesey Antiquarian Society Transactions (1914)

The Visiting Fairy

Mary Roberts, of Newborough, used to receive visits once a week from a little woman who used to bring her a loaf of bread in return for the loan of her gridiron (gradell) for baking bread. The Fairy always told her not to look after her when she left the house, but one day she transgressed, and took a peep as the Fairy went away. The latter went straight to the lake – Llyn Rhosddu – near the house at Newborough, and plunged into its waters and disappeared. This took place about a century ago.

Elias Owen: 'Welsh Folklore' (1887)

Transportation

An examination of the Anglesey Quarter Sessions files reveals that three cases involved transportation (to the American colonies) prior to 1775/6 and the rest relate to sentences of transportation imposed between 1807 and 1849/50. All the offences (felonies) concerned property rather than violence to the person, i.e. to the stealing of livestock or to housebreaking and the theft of clothing or household items (including food). In 1820, John Hughes and Catherine Ellis were sentenced at the Great Sessions to death but these sentences were commuted to ones of 14 years' transportation. Captain Thomas Jones of the brig *Esther* contracted for

£30) to convey these two convicts to London. William Jones was sentenced to transportation for life at the Great Sessions in 1829 for stealing sheep (five ewes and five wethers) and removed to the *Justitia* at Woolwich. In 1840, William Williams (Llangadwaladr) and Griffith Jones (Trefdraeth), both labourers, though Jones was also said to be a National School master, received life sentences (commuted to ten years) for stealing a ram valued at 35s. John and Hugh Thomas were sentenced to seven years' transportation in 1842 for house-breaking. The items stolen were: four silk handkerchiefs (value 5s.), two loaves of barley bread (6d.), two loaves of bread (6d.) and six pounds of bread (6d.), the property of one Rowland Williams. In short, the offences were quite typical, a pathetic catalogue of minor crimes, in modern terms – the sad case of Anne Williams, otherwise Edwards, for example, aged 17, of Llanfechell, who was convicted of housebreaking and sentenced to ten years' transportation in 1842 at the Spring Assizes at Beaumaris. Anne, who was undefended, claimed that the items alleged to have been stolen – 'two cotton gowns, a pair of stays, a silk handkerchief, and several other articles of wearing apparel' – had been given to her by the householder, Thomas Hughes of Llanfechell (and brother of the owner-prosecutrix) and that he had offered her, on a later occasion, 'a merino dress' which she had refused. She had no witnesses of his giving her the clothes but 'plenty could speak of his being in the habit of visiting her'. Yet no witnesses to the latter 'responded to her call'. Thomas Hughes may have had something to hide here but Anne Williams *alias* Edwards admitted to a previous conviction for felony and her fate was sealed. She later sailed to Van Diemen's Land aboard the transport *Garland Grove* to serve her sentence. She was freed, it seems, in 1853 and the rest of her story is unknown.

Lewis Lloyd: 'Australians From Wales' (1988)

An Occasion of Immorality

Up to within recent years some very old Customs and Usages survived in the Island in various forms, and a few survive to the present day.

Down to the latter end of the last century there existed what was called 'Gwylmabsant' which was held in different places, such as Trefdraeth, Penmynydd, and other central neighbourhoods. At first, as the name (which means 'the feast of the saint's son') indicates, this institution was of a religious character, and perhaps of a religious origin, and object; but in the course of time it deteriorated to such a degree that it became an occasion of immorality, and great efforts were made to put it down. These 'Gwyliau' were also used as hiring fairs. The hiring fair of Penmynydd was announced in Almanacs and so on for many years after it was discontinued. On these fair days, interludes or stage entertainments were very common. They were a kind of dramas acted in the open air, as suitable buildings for the purpose were not to be had at that time. They conformed in character with the public taste. They were not very elevating it must be admitted excepting only the productions of Twm o'r Nant which show much talent, and hold a respectable place in the literature of Wales.

W. Pritchard
in the Anglesey Antiquarian Society Transactions (1914)

Penmynydd

Penmynydd, a house between Llangefni and Porthaethwy, was the home of Owain Tudur. He became a member of the court of Henry V and when the king died married his widow, Queen Catherine, Catherine of Valoise in France, who was immortalised by Shakespeare in a courting scene. Visiting Penmynydd with her new husband she found his cousins to be 'the goodliest dumb creatures'.

I reached Penmynydd a small village consisting of a few white houses and a mill. The meaning of Penmynydd is literally the top of a hill. The village does not stand on a hill, but the church which is at some distance, stands on one, or rather on a hillock. And it is probable from the circumstance of the church standing on a hillock, that the parish derives its name. Towards the church after a slight glance at the village, I proceeded with hasty steps, and was soon at the foot of the hillock. A house, that of the clergyman, stands near the church, on the top of the hill. I opened a gate, and entered a lane which seemed to lead up to the church.

As I was passing some low buildings, probably offices pertaining to the house, a head was thrust from a doorway, which stared at me. It was a strange hirsute head, and probably looked more strange and hirsute than it naturally was, owing to its having a hairy cap upon it.

'Good day,' said I.

'Good days, sar,' said the head, and in a moment more a man of middle stature, about fifty, in hairy cap, shirt-sleeves, and green apron round his waist, stood before me. He looked the beau-ideal of a servant of all work.

'Can I see the church?' said I.

'Ah, you want to see the church,' said honest Scrub. 'Yes, sar!' you shall see the church. You go up road there past church – come to house, knock at door – say what you want – and nice little girl show you church. Ah, you quite right to come and see church – fine tomb there and clebber man sleeping in it with his wife, clebber man that – Owen Tiddir; married great queen – dyn clebber iawn.'

Following the suggestions of the man of the hairy cap I went round the church and knocked at the door of the house, a handsome parsonage. A nice little servant-girl presently made her appearance at the door, of whom I inquired whether I could see the church.

'Certainly, sir,' said she; 'I will go for the key and accompany you.'

She fetched the key and away we went to the church. It is a venerable chapel-like edifice, with a belfry towards the west; the roof, sinking by two gradations, is lower at the eastern or altar end, than at the other. The girl, unlocking the door, ushered me into the interior.

'Which is the tomb of Tudor?' said I to the pretty damsel.

'There it is, sir,' said she, pointing to the north side of the church; 'there is the tomb of Owen Tudor.'

Beneath a low-roofed arch lay sculptured in stone, on an altar tomb, the figures of a man and woman; that of the man in armour; that of the woman in graceful drapery. The male figure lay next the wall.

'And you think,' said I to the girl, 'that yonder figure is that of Owen Tudor?'

'Yes sir,' said the girl; 'yon figure is that of Owen Tudor; the other is that of his wife, the great queen; both their bodies rest below.'

I forbore to say that the figures were not those of Owen Tudor and the great queen, his wife; and I forbore to say that their bodies did not rest in that church, nor anywhere in the neighbourhood, for I was unwilling to dispel a pleasing delusion. The tomb is doubtless a tomb of one of the Tudor race, and of a gentle partner of his, but not of the Rose of Mona and Catharine of France. Her bones rest in some corner of Westminster's noble abbey; his moulder amongst those of thousands of others, Yorkis's and Lancastrians, under the surface of the plain, where Mortimer's Cross once stood, that plain on the eastern side of which meanders the murmuring Lug; that noble plain, where one of the hardest battles which ever blooded English soil was fought; where beautiful young Edward gained a crown, and old Owen lost a head, which when young had been the most beautiful of heads, which had gained for him the appellation of the Rose of Anglesey, and which had captivated the glances of the fair daughter of France, the widow of Monmouth's Harry, the immortal victor of Agincourt.

George Borrow: 'Wild Wales' (1862)

The Crigyll Robbers

Near Rhosneigr in Anglesey, home since the late 1770s of a thriving ship-building industry, gangs of wreckers called the Wreckers of Crigyll flourished at various periods, particularly during the Eighteenth Century. They became notorious for their activities at luring ships to their doom and then plundering them, so much so that long after the original 'gang' which gave these wreckers their name had met its fate, wrecks were still being attributed to its activities.

On 30 October 1867, *The Times* declared that: 'The wreck (of the *Earl of Chester*) is now a prey to the notorious wreckers of the coast known to Welsh seafaring men as Lladron Crigyll (*the Crigyll robbers*). Many hundreds of them were there yesterday stealing whatever they could carry away.'

The original 'gang', though, was active as early as 1715, when in fact its members were brought to trial. It is on record that: 'On Tuesday 25 April, 1715, at the County Gaol, Beaumaris, were committed for felony three men, known as the Lladron Creigiau Crigyll (*the robbers of Crigyll rocks*), who were found guilty of plundering the wreck of the sloop called *The Charming Jenny* stranded at Crigyll.'

Those were days of harsh punishments, when even the theft of a loaf of bread was a hanging offence, and it is very probable that this little band of wreckers met with a sad though not undeserved end. Another writer of roughly the same period noted of a different wreck: ' . . . the owner . . . is come here, and is going to hang half a dozen of the Thieves who rob'd the wreck.'

Another band of Crigyll wreckers – Owen John Ambrose of Llanfihangel-yn-Nhywyn, Gabriel Roberts of Ceirchiog, Thomas Roberts of Llanfaelog and Hugh Griffith Hughes, also of Llanfaelog – were more fortunate. They were tried in April, 1741, at Beaumaris Assizes, before Mr Justice Martyn. All were accused of robbing a Liverpool brigantine, the *Loveday & Betty*, which had been driven onshore and stranded by the south-westerly gales of 31 December, 1740. Once again, the penalty they faced for felony was the noose, and the trial attracted such a lot of attention that many notable businessmen travelled to Beaumaris to attend it.

One of these, William Bulkeley, recorded in his diary: 'Tho this is the last day of the Sessions the Court sat to try causes till 3 in the Evening; a thing never known before in the history of man. Martyn the Judge being every day drunk deferred all business to the last, when they were hustled over in a very unbecoming manner.'

Much to the horror of everyone, including a gentleman called Lewis Morris (father of William Morris), Judge Martyn remained in such a drunken state that he discharged all the prisoners, notwithstanding the fact that they were obviously guilty. In a poem which was to become a popular ballad everywhere, Lewis Morris passionately declaimed against their freedom and spoke of the hanging he insisted they had deserved. The following extract gives us some idea of how strongly the people of the coast felt about the unholy deeds of the wreckers:

'How fine to the good and honest
Is the light of candle and fire;
How fine to the brigands of the night
Is to be in darkened houses;
How fine to my ears is it to hear
Of the hanging of the Thieves of Crigyll.

It is a village without the fear of God,
Where evil lives in the hearts of men,
Bandits of the waves, vicious villains
Hiding their lanterns under their cloaks;
May God keep innocent travellers
From wrecking on the rocks of Crigyll.'

Dilys Gater: 'Historic Shipwrecks of Wales' (1992)

A Melancholy Event

In the month of December 1785 the Abermenai boat in going from Caernarvon was swamped in the opposite sand-bank, and all the passengers perished except one, Mr Hugh Williams, a respectable farmer now living at Tyn Llwydan near Aberfraw. The unaffected narrative of the later melancholy event I received from Mr Williams himself, and his story is too interesting to be related in any other than his own words:

'The Abermenai ferry-boat usually leaves Caernarvon on the return of the tide, but the 5th December, being the fair day, the boat did not leave that evening until near four o'clock, and the wind which blew strong from the south-east was right upon our starboard bow. It was necessary that the boat should be kept in close to the Caernarvonshire side, not only that we might have the benefit of the channel, which runs near the shore, but also we might be sheltered from the wind, which blew directly towards two sandbanks, at that time divided by a channel called 'The Shifting Sands'. It was not long before I perceived that the boat was not kept sufficiently in the channel, and I immediately told a friend of my apprehensions that we were approaching too near the bank. He agreed and we requested the ferry men to use their best efforts to keep her off. Every exertion was made with the oars, for we had no sail, but without effect, for we soon grounded upon the sandbank. Alarmed at our situation, as it was nearly low water some of the strongest and tallest of the passengers leapt into the water and, with their joint force, endeavoured to thrust the boat off. This, however, was to no purpose, for every time they moved her from the spot she was with violence driven back. In this distressing situation the boat half filled with water, with a heavy sea breaking over us, we thought it best to quit her and remain on the bank in hope, before the rising again of the tide. Almost the moment we had quitted her she filled with water and swamped. Before leaving her, however, I took the precaution of securing the mast on which, in case of necessity, I resolved to attempt my escape. On this I was carried to a part of the bank nearest the Anglesey shore where I observed my friend with one of the oars, which he had secured for a similar purpose. We were fifty five in number, including women and children, that can best be conceived than described. Exposed on a quick sand in a cold night, to all the horrors of premature death which we knew without assistance must be certain on the return of the tide. Our only remaining hope was that we should make our distress known. We accordingly united our voices in repeated cries for assistance and were heard. The alarm bell was rung and, tempestuous as the night was, several boats put off to our assistance. Our hopes were now high that we should shortly be rescued from the impending danger. But our spirits were dashed when we discovered that they dare not approach us on the bank lest a similar fate should befall them. Danger was with the passing of every moment increasing, and I decided in desperation to quit the bank and trust myself to the mercy of the sea. Being a good swimmer I felt confident that, with the mast, I should be able to gain the Anglesey shore. I found my friend with the oar and suggested that we should tie the mast and the oar together with two straw ropes and put our trust in these. I fastened them together, but my friend had not fortitude enough to come with me. I determined, therefore to make the effort alone. I pulled off my boots and greatcoat so as not to be impeded and we bade each other a fairwell. I pushed my raft a little off the bank and placed myself upon it, but at that moment it turned round and threw me underneath. In this position, with one of my arms flung through the rope, and using all my strength to keep my head above water, I was carried off the bank. When I had been in the water about an hour I spotted a light at a considerable distance. This I believed to be Tal y Voel ferry house. My drooping spirits were revived and I made every effort to make the shore by pushing the raft towards it, at the same time calling out loudly for help. But you may imagine my dissapointment when, in spite of everything, I was carried past the light and found myself driving on rapidly, before the wind and tide, deprived now of every hope of being rescued. Dreadful as was my situation. I still had strength enough to perservere in my efforts to gain the shore. These, after being for some time beaten about by the surge carrying me back into the water, were effectual. I was thus retrieved from almost inevitable death. Exerting myself to the utmost I crawled towards the place where I had seen the light, distant at least a mile from me, but was obliged to rest and lie under a hedge till my strength was recovered. The rain and wind soon roused me, and after repeated struggles I reached Tal y Voel ferry house. I was first seen by a female of the family who immediately ran screaming under the impression that she had encountered a ghost. The family, by this means, were roused and I was taken into the house. They put me into a warm bed, gave me some brandy and applied heated bricks to my extremities; this treatment had a good effect and on the following morning no other unpleasant sensation was left than that of extreme debility. Having been married but a very short time, I determined to be the welcome messenger to my wife of my own deliverance. I therefore hastened home as early as possible, and had the good fortune to find that the news of the melancholy event had not yet reached my dwelling . . . The morning presented a spectacle along the shore which I cannot attempt to describe. Several of the bodies had been cast up during the night. The friends of the sufferers crowded the banks and the agitated inquiries of relatives concerning loved ones whose fate was doubtful or unknown fill me with horror when I recall them. I was the only survivor of this melancholy event. Besides the bodies thrown upon the shore by the tide, so many were found in various positions sunk in the sand bank, and it was some time before their corpses could be dug out. The boat was never recovered and is supposed to be even yet lodged in the bank.'

William Bingley: 'North Wales: Scenery, Antiquities, Customs' (1804)

Island to Island

Whilst smuggling was practised throughout the eighteenth century in the St George's Channel and the Irish Sea, it was probably in mid-century that it was at its height. Until 1765 the Isle of Man was constitutionally independent of the English Crown; it was privately owned and not subject to the Customs duties or laws of England. As taxes on the mainland increased under the pressure of continental wars, so the Isle of Man became more and more popular as a storehouse for high duty goods, tobacco, rum, brandy and gin, in particular, which were distributed as convenient to the mainland. All the smugglers had to do was to wait for their opportunity for sailing with a favourable wind, making preferably for a quiet strip of beach. One has only to look at a chart to recognize how suitable Anglesey and the North Wales coast were for the smugglers' purposes, coming from the Isle of Man or Ireland, as indeed the pirates of the sixteenth and seventeenth centuries had done before them. On 30 April 1765, the Isle of Man was purchased with £70,000 of Customs money, and became subject to the same laws as the rest of England and Wales. The letters which had passed between the Collector of Customs at Beaumaris and the Board of Commissioners of Customs between January 1763 and March 1767 are, of considerable interest, and form the main source for the paragraphs which follow.

The letters tell the story of smuggling as seen through the eys of those who tried to prevent it: the Collector, in charge of the port, a post of considerable antiquity and ever increasing complexity; the Comptroller, who although otherwise subordinate to the Collector, had joint responsibility with him for the cash and accounts of the port; the preventive service afloat; the Commanders of the Revenue cruisers who had to battle against both the smugglers and the elements, for the smugglers often operated in foul weather hoping to evade detection; and finally the shore-based Tide-Surveyors, Tide-Waiters, Land-Surveyors and Land-Waiters, the riding officers and the boatmen. Captain William Gambold, master of the Revenue cutter *Pelham*, based for most of this time at Beaumaris, outlined in a letter to the Board of Commissioners in May 1763 some of the problems which confronted him and his men. He alleged that the smugglers got passage to the Isle of Man from Liverpool 'or the first place they can find boats bound there'; at the Isle of Man, 'several of the smugglers joyn together and hire an Irish wherry of thirty or forty tons with 9 or 10 hands on board, in which they bring over their prohibited goods, and do not come near the shore till about twelve o'clock at night.' Once they approached a beach, they had rapid cooperation from the dwellers ashore: 'in less than an hour's time (they) will land and carry the whole cargo into the country, as there are several farmers concern'd with them, which have their cart's and horses ready for that purpose.' Gambold stated that some of the Irish vessels which plied between the Isle of Man and the Welsh coast were not engaged in any trade but smuggling, and were built 'slight and sharp' so that they were 'remarkable fast sailers.' Moreover, when his Revenue cutter approached the places where he suspected the smugglers were landing their goods, 'the smugglers on shore make fire on the hills for a signal to the wherrys that we are on that coast, so that they may avoide us.'

Aled Eames: 'Ships and Seamen of Anglesey' (1973)

The Rothsay Castle Tragedy

One of the most notorious wrecks off the Welsh coast which became tragically disastrous due in a large part to lack of safety precautions and sea-worthiness of the vessel itself, was that of the *Rothsay Castle*, a paddle-steamer which plied a day-trip trade between Liverpool and Beaumaris. On August 18, 1831, in bad weather, she went aground on Dutchman's Bank in Beaumaris Bay, and broke her back.

The vessel had originally been built to serve along the Clyde, and when she arrived in Liverpool, she was already a tired, underpowered ship which should never have put to sea again. In fact, it is reported that several of the prospective crew refused point blank to sail in her – and one of them later had this refusal accepted by the Manchester Commissioners in Lunacy as undisputable proof that the man had been sane at the time.

Apart from material facts that the ship's only boat had no oars and a hole in the bottom, that there was no signal gun, and that the timbers were rotting, it was common knowledge among the sea-going fraternity that this vessel was far from seaworthy. In addition, rumour had it that the officers were quarrelsome and often drunk. But unfortunately, most of these grave drawbacks were not evident to the 150 day-trippers who crowded on board on that fateful morning of August 17, and felt the ship judder beneath them when she headed out to sea round about mid-day.

Once at sea, the *Rothsay Castle* took the full force of strong winds and heavy seas, and soon even the bandsmen who had been playing for the pleasure of the passengers, were crippled with sea-sickness. The passengers were, not surprisingly, becoming increasingly alarmed and a deputation went below to request the captain to return to Liverpool. They were met, however, with horrible oaths and instructions to keep out and stop interfering, from a captain who was well and truly drunk.

By 5 o'clock, when Captain Atkinson at last came on deck, the ship was letting in water. He had no more useful contribution to make to the wellbeing of the passengers, however, than to say darkly that 'This night will tell a tale', and allow the poor *Rothsay Castle* to plod on in the heavy seas. By ten o'clock in the evening, the ship passed the Great Orme – a mere thirty-six miles from their starting-place in Liverpool – but those aboard who were hoping to make Beaumaris very shortly had their hopes dashed when, within sight of Puffin Island, one of the firemen came on deck to report two feet of water in the stokehold.

Unless the ship was to run out of steam, somebody had to man the pumps – so the long-suffering passengers were ordered below. The pumps, however, like so many other things on the ship, did not work, so in desperation, the male passengers tried to form a chain and bail the water out with buckets. This bright idea was soon squashed when they were informed that the only bucket on the ship had fallen overboard.

What might have seemed farcical in the extreme, however, soon turned to real tragedy when the ship was caught on the Dutchman's Bank. The captain once again displayed his shiftlessness in a position of command and his propensity for blaming others whenever things went wrong; he cursed the helmsman, claiming that the latter had never known how to steer, and then, notwithstanding that the fires were out below so that there was no steam, he ordered the ship 'full astern'. Since she was not able to answer to any orders at all, she continued to bump on across the treacherous sands that formed the Dutchman's Bank for another mile or so. Then she began to break up.

The funnel was first to go, taking the main-mast along with it. The side of the ship was smashed in, and the captain was among those swept to their death. Many of the passengers had been lashed to the mast for safety, and were unable to escape – it was a terrible end to what had begun as a pleasure trip with the band playing and the bunting flying.

There were only twenty-three survivors of the wreck. Nine of them, including one lone woman, drifted on what remained of the poop, using the lady's skirts as a sail. Others clung to pieces of wreckage. When morning came and the terrible plight of the *Rothsay Castle* could be seen from the shore, boats put out to pick up the survivors, but there was on this occasion no lifeboat that might have come to the assistance of the doomed ship.

As a result of the tragedy, however, the Anglesey Lifesaving

Association set up a lifeboat station at Penmon in the following year, and in response to an application to the Government, a new lighthouse was built at Penmon, completed in 1838.

Dilys Gater: 'Historic Shipwrecks in Wales' (1992)

The Royal Charter

When we think of Dickens we tend to view him primarily as the supreme master of English fiction. But he also wrote a prolific number of articles for periodicals, and following the terrible tragedy of the Royal Charter off the northern coast of Ynys Môn in 1859 he visited Moelfre and Llanallgo in order to record his impressions, and these were later incorporated in his book The Uncommercial Traveller.

The 'Royal Charter' was returning from Australia with both gold and passengers when she ran into very severe weather conditions. When the ship began to break up on the rocky Ynys Môn coastline it was quickly realised that there was little or no hope. Out of total of approximately 490 people on board only forty survived. For a matter of weeks afterwards bodies were washed ashore. Many were taken to the vicarage at Llanallgo, where the Rev. Stephen Roose Hughes supervised the identification of the dead, and arranged for the next of kin to be traced and informed of their bereavement. Dickens developed an enormous admiration for Hughes, whose health began to suffer as a result of the stress he experienced at that time.

It is interesting to note that 'The Royal Charter' was launched in Sandycroft in Flintshire in August 1855. Another great novelist, this time an American one, Nathaniel Hawthorne, who is also represented in this anthology, has left a detailed account of the launch in his English Notebook. ' . . . when we expected to see her plunge into the Dee,' he writes, 'she came to a full stop . . . this noble ship was stuck fast in the mud of the Dee, and without deepening the bed of the river, I do not see how her vast iron hulk is ever to be got out.'

That very morning I had come bowling down, and struggling up, hill-country roads; looking back at snowy summits; meeting courteous peasants well to do, driving fat pigs and cattle to market: noting the neat and thrifty dwellings, with their unusual quantity of clean white linen, drying on the bushes; having windy weather suggested by every cotter's little rick, with its thatch straw-ridged and extra straw-ridged into overlapping compartments like the back of a rhincoeros. Had I not given a lift of fourteen miles to the Coast-guardsman (kit and all), who was coming to his spell of duty there, and had we not just now parted company? So it was; but the journey seemed to glide down into the placid sea, with other chafe and trouble, and for the moment nothing was so calmly and monotonously real under the sunlight as the gentle rising and falling of the water with its freight, the regular turning of the windlass aboard the Lighter, and the slight obstruction so very near my feet.

O reader, haply turning this page by the fireside at Home, and hearing the night wind rumble in the chimney, that slight obstruction was the uppermost fragment of the Wreck of the *Royal Charter*, Australian trader and passenger ship, homeward bound, that struck here on the terrible morning of the twenty-sixth of this October, broke into three parts, went down with her treasure of at least five hundred human lives, and has never stirred since!

From which point, or from which, she drove ashore, stern foremost; on which side, or on which, she passed the little Island in the bay, for ages henceforth to be aground certain yards outside her; these are rendered bootless questions by the darkness of that night and the darkness of death. Here she went down.

Even as I stood on the beach with the words 'Here she went down!' in my ears, a diver in his grotesque dress, dipped heavily over the side of the boat alongside the Lighter, and dropped to the bottom.

Only two short months had gone, since a man, living on the nearest hill-top overlooking the sea, being blown out of bed at about daybreak by the wind that had begun to strip his root off, and getting upon a ladder with his nearest neighbour to construct some temporary device for keeping his house over his head, saw from the ladder's elevation as he looked down by chance towards the shore, some dark troubled object close in with the land. And he and the other, descending to the beach, and finding the sea mercilessly beating over a great broken ship, had clambered up the stony ways, like staircases without stairs, on which the wild village hangs in little clusters, as fruit hangs on boughs, and had given the alarm. And so, over the hill-slopes, and past the waterfall, and down the gullies where the land drains off into the ocean, the scattered quarrymen and fisher-men inhabiting that part of Wales had come running to the dismal sight – their clergyman among them. And as they stood in the leaden morning, stricken with pity, leaning hard against the wind, their breath and vision often failing as the sleet and spray rushed at them from the ever forming and dissolving mountains of sea, and as the wool which was a part of the vessel's cargo blew in with the salt foam and remained upon the land when the foam melted, they saw the ship's life-boat put off from one of the heaps of wreck; and first, there were three men in her, and in a moment she capsized, and there were but two;

and again, she was struck by a vast mass of water, and there was but one; and again, she was thrown bottom upward, and that one, with his arm struck through the broken planks and waving as if for the help that could never reach him, went down into the deep.

It was the clergyman himself from whom I heard this, while I stood on the shore, looking in his kind wholesome face as it turned to the spot where the boat had been. The divers were down then, and busy. They were 'lifting' to-day the gold found yesterday – some five-and-twenty thousand pounds. Of three hundred and fifty thousand pounds' worth of gold, three hundred thousands pounds' worth, in round numbers, was at that time recovered. The great bulk of the remainder was surely and steadily coming up. Some loss of sovereigns there would be, of course; indeed, at first sovereigns had drifted in with the sand, and been scattered far and wide over the beach, like sea-shells.

He had the church keys in his hand, and opened the churchyard gate, and opened the church door; and we went in.

It is a little church of great antiquity; there is reason to believe that some church has occupied the spot, these thousand years or more. The pulpit was gone, and other things usually belonging to the church were gone, owing to its living congregation having deserted it for the neighbouring school-room, and yielded it up to the dead. The very Commandments had been shouldered out of their places, in the bringing in of the dead; the black wooden tables on which they were painted, were askew, and on the stone pavement below them, and on the stone pavement all over the church, were the marks and stains where the drowned had been laid down. The eye, with little or no aid from the imagination, could yet see how the bodies had been turned, and where the head had been and where the feet. Some faded traces of the wreck of the Australian ship may be discernible on the stone pavement of this little church, hundreds of years hence, when the digging for gold in Australia shall have long and long ceased out of the land.

Forty-four shipwrecked men and women lay here at one time, awaiting burial. Here, with weeping and wailing in every room of his house, my companion worked alone for hours, solemnly surrounded by eyes that could not see him, and by lips that could not speak to him, patiently examining the tattered clothing, cutting off buttons, hair, marks from linen, anything that might lead to subsequent identification, studying faces, looking for a scar, a bent finger, a crooked toe, comparing letters sent to him with the ruin about him. 'My dearest brother had bright grey eyes and a pleasant simle,' one sister wrote. 'O poor sister! well for you to be far from here, and keep that as your last remembrance of him!'

The ladies of the clergyman's family, his wife and two sisters-in-law, came in among the bodies often. It grew to be the business of their lives to do so. Any new arrival of a bereaved woman would stimulate their pity to compare the description brought, with the dread realities. Sometimes, they would go back able to say, 'I have found him,' or, 'I think she lies there.' Perhaps, the mourner, unable to bear the sight of all that lay in the church, would be led in blindfold. Conducted to the spot with many compassionate words, and encouraged to look, she would say, with a piercing cry, 'This is my boy!' and drop insensible on the insensible figure.

From the church, we passed out into the churchyard. Here, there lay, at that time, one hundred and forty-five bodies, that had come ashore from the wreck. He had buried them, when not identified, in graves containing four each. He had numbered each body in a register describing it, and had placed a corresponding number on each coffin, and over each grave. Identified bodies he had buried singly, in private graves, in another part of the churchyard. Several bodies had been exhumed from the graves of four, as relatives had come from a distance and seen his register; and, when recognised, these have been reburied in private graves, so that the mourners might erect separate headstones over the remains. In all such cases he had performed the funeral service a second time, and the ladies of his house had attended. There had been no offence in the poor ashes when they were brought again to the light of day; the beneficent Earth had already absorbed it. The drowned were buried in their clothes. To supply the great sudden demand for coffins, he had got all the neighbouring people handy at tools, to work the livelong day, and Sunday likewise. The coffins were neatly formed; – I had seen two, waiting for occupants, under the lee of the ruined walls of a stone hut on the beach, within call of the tent where the Christmas Feast was held. Similarly, one of the graves for four was lying open and ready, here, in the churchyard. So much of the scanty space was already devoted to the wrecked people, that the villagers had begun to express uneasy doubts whether they themselves could lie in their own ground, with their forefathers and descendants, by-and-by. The churchyard being but a step from the clergyman's dwelling-house, we crossed to the latter; the white surplice was hanging up near the door ready to be put on at any time, for a funeral service.

In this noble modesty, in this beautiful simplicity, in this serene avoidance of the least attempt to 'improve' an occasion which might be supposed to have sunk of its own weight into my heart, I seemed to have happily come, in a few steps, from the churchyard with its open grave, which was the type of Death, to the Christian dwelling side by side with it, which was the type of Resurrection. I never shall think of the former, without the latter. The two will always rest side by side in my memory. If I had lost any one dear to me in this unfortunate ship, if I had made a voyage from Australia to look at the grave in the churchyard, I should go away, thankful to God that that house was so close to it, and that its shadow by day and its domestic lights by night fell upon the earth in which its Master had so tenderly laid my dear one's head.

Charles Dickens: 'The Uncommercial Traveller' (1860)

Wreck of the Royal Charter

*(The vicar of Penrhos Lligwy is said to have died as a
result of strain and overwork after the wreck.)*

He gave, to begin with, his duty.
The appropriate words
Written out in a hundred letters:
'Dear madam . . . he did not suffer,'
'Your daughter is with God,'
'The loss was rapid;
They cannot have felt much pain.'

What else could he write?
That the wreck had taken hours?
That slowly they saw their hopes
Destroyed, and knew
All of the horror of dying?
That Tom from the shop
Had drowned while his father watched
Ten yards away?

He gave, to begin with, his duty,
Assuming command;
Wrote letters, saw relatives,
Presided at funerals; tried
Preserving the souls of his flock
From a hundred sins,
And the wrath of an ignorant world.

In the end he was giving too much:
He died of the wreck,
Drowned in the wash of their deaths,
In the deeps of their fear,
Giving comfort to others,
Who, having no knowledge of death,
Had no need of the comfort he gave.

Sally Roberts Jones from 'Turning Away' (1969)

Learning Their Seamanship

A number of Moelfre residents remember the *Tryfan* bringing coal to Moelfre beach, and the fun and laughter enjoyed by the village lads during the unloading. Many of these lads and their forefathers learnt their seamanship on the coastal ships before moving to the larger ships at Liverpool, and I well remember the late Captain Harry Roberts, Moelfre describing his early days on the *Dinas* and the *Sara* sailing from Afon Menai to the beaches of Ynys Môn, and how, after becoming captain of his own ship, he would be paid extra for the freight if he unloaded on a dangerous beach such as Traeth Swtan where the westerly winds made it difficult to kedge out. This, of course, explains why there are so many iron rings attached to the rocks on many a small beach where the ships used to dry out, rings securing ropes and for warping. Unloading on open beaches straight into the farmers' carts, – this was a trade followed by hundreds of Welsh ships, and the pattern was very similar along the coast from the river Dee to the Bristol Channel. Owain Roberts illustrated in an exceptionally interesting article in *Cymru a'r Môr/Maritime Wales* how the small sloop, the *Darling* (built on the shores of the river Mawddach) sailed for over a hundred years in the Irish Sea, carrying potatoes from Ireland and, for over fifty years, stone from Traeth Bychan, Môn to build the cob at Caergybi (*Holyhead*).

A good example of the problems that were likely to arise during a voyage along the coast is illustrated in verses written in his own natural dialect by a sailor from Môn (*Anglesey*), Dick Pritchard, mate of the *Pickavance*, a small coal-burning coaster. The verses give an account of one voyage in December 1920, when Captain Hugh Griffiths, Amlwch was her captain. She left Liverpool in favourable weather but was caught by strong winds near Pwynt Leinws (*Point Lynas*) and once the *Pickavance* had moved away from the shelter of Ynys Môn (*Anglesey*) she could make but little headway because of the wind and high sea and had to turn back for shelter in Moelfre. Having sheltered at Moelfre for a few hours, however, the very factor that has accounted for so many shipwrecks in this bay happened. The wind went round suddenly to the north, as in the case of the *Royal Charter* and the *Hindlea*, and the ship, close to the rocks and bereft of any shelter, eventually lost her anchor. In the days of sailing ships, many ships finding themselves in the same situation would not have survived, and that is why so many sailors have been saved by the renowned lifeboatmen of Moelfre. But in the case of the *Pickavance* her engines saved the day for Captain Griffiths, who decided to press on, and eventually gained the port of Caergybi.

Aled Eames: 'Shrouded Quays' (1991)

The Whalers of Anglesey

In 1936 one third of the registered workforce of Anglesey was unemployed. The shipping industry in particular was suffering from the consequences of the economic depression of the 1930s. For generations the young men from Anglesey, especially those from Holyhead, Amlwch, Cemaes and Moelfre, had found work with the shipping lines. But in 1936 there were very few vacancies on foreign going ships, and even the L.M.S. cross-channel ferries and cargo-boats at Holyhead could only provide limited casual employment at certain times of the year. Assistance, however, arrived from an unexpected quarter: from the whaling industry.

In the 1930s Lever Brothers & Unilever Limited through a subsidiary company, The Southern Whaling & Sealing Company Limited, operated a whaling fleet in the Antarctic. The crews of their factory ships and whale chasers were virtually all Norwegian. In fact the Norwegians monopolised most of the skilled trades of the whaling industry. But in 1936 the Norwegians overplayed their hand when they boycotted the Unilever ships that were being repaired in Sondefjord, Norway. In retaliation Unilever transferred their ships to Newcastle for the annual overhaul. They also decided that since the ships were British owned British seamen should have the opportunity of sailing in them. They had in effect grasped the first chance given to them of breaking the Norwegian stranglehold on the industry. An agreement was reached between the British and Norwegian governments that the factory ships, which each carried a crew of approximately three hundred men, would be one third British. One hundred fishermen from the East coast of Britain were promptly recruited for that purpose. Two Welshmen on the staff of Unilever, Mr Clement Edward Davies a director of Lever Brothers & Unilever Limited and Mr T.H. Humphreys the managing director of The Southern Whaling & Sealing Co., Ltd., decided to go even further afield and enlist young men from the Welsh ports. Captain William Williams of Primrose Villa, Morfa Nefyn, who was the superintendent of the whaling company, was instructed to recruit the Welsh whalers.

Captain Williams contacted Mr William Owen, a Trinity House pilot, who lived at 8, Hibernia Row, Holyhead, asking him whether he knew of any Anglesey men interested in joining the 1936/37 whaling expedition. Mr Owen replied that he knew many unemployed men in the county who would welcome work of any description.

After he had been approached by Captain Williams, Wil Owen Pilot, puffing his pipe as usual – it was hardly ever out of his mouth – called at the Labour Exchange offices in William Street, and asked one of the officials if they were interested in finding work for the unemployed men of Holyhead on the factory ships belonging to Unilever. One of the officials replies, 'Can't you read that sign?' Wil Owen looked at it. It was a 'No Smoking' sign. The Labour Exchange officials had not been directly approached by Unilever, so they were not interested. The correct procedure had not been adopted, so they looked the other way.

Not quite knowing how to proceed after that rebuff Wil Owen allowed Captain Williams to establish his headquarters in his terraced house in Hibernia Row. It was there that Captain Williams worked, ate, and slept during his recruiting campaign of 1936, although he also occasionally stayed at the Station Hotel.

For the 1936/37 whaling season they succeeded in enlisting twenty men and four boys from Holyhead, sixteen men from Amlwch, two from Cemaes, and two from Moelfre. A total of forty four men and boys eventually left Anglesey to sail on the whaling factory ships, the *Southern Empress* and the *Southern Princess*. During the voyage one or two of those who had been to sea before were transferred on to the catchers.

When the Anglesey whalers returned home from the Antarctic in the spring of 1937 their favourable reports on the food, pay and conditions of service fired the imagination of the unemployed men of the county, who resolved to follow their example if the opportunity ever arose.

Alun Owen: 'The Whalers of Anglesey' (1983)

Rivalry

By a happy chance, when I was a boy in the twenties and thirties, I had close relatives on my mother's side at Holyhead and on my father's at Morfa Nefyn and my brothers and I spent many happy holidays exploring with our cousins the different delights and pleasures of each place.

At Holyhead we soon established a look out post in one of the attics which commanded a wide view of the harbour from which we keenly watched for arrivals and departures, we hung about the harbour to observe the berthing of the *Scotia*, *Hibernia* or *Cambria*, the noisy and dusty process of coaling ship from the attendant barge with its endless bucket-chain elevator which shot the coal into a chute down which it rattled into the bunkers, the warping of the ship from the arrival to the departure side of the harbour, and between whiles we would patrol the station platforms to make sure that the Irish Mail, headed by the superb new Royal Scot engine in its maroon livery, departed at the correct time. I have a feeling that the whole routine of meal times in my aunt's household revolved around train and boat departures for the period of our stay.

The holiday at Morfa Nefyn was utterly different; naturally we spent a lot of time on the beach, but we also walked a great deal, along the cliffs to Nefyn, or over the golf course and on to Abergeirch where the Irish telegraph cable came ashore; we climbed Garn Boduan or Garn Fadryn to enjoy views of the whole Lleyn peninsula and distant Bardsey laid out before us, and, of course, we explored around Porthdinllaen, the lifeboat house and the old SS *Dora* warehouse, played in and among the beached boats, and once, a great thrill in 1933 or thereabouts, in a wrecked RAF flying boat. It was about this time that I heard for the first time that if justice had been properly done, Porthdinllaen and not Holyhead would have become the packet station for Ireland, and that Porthdinllaen lost the contest by only one vote in Parliament. It seemed a simple story about a single, rather sad, event.

M. Ellis-Williams: 'Packet to Ireland' (1984)

Patchworks

of Amlwch,
a pattern of fields and buildings
interlocking with lives.

I have chosen
a folk pattern,
forsaking isolation

an interminable quilt,
joined to responses and influences
in conflict and agreement
changing subtly with changes in history
the growth of poems
the retreat of peoples
personal defeat and victory.

I have chosen
the use of available material,
a feature of the passing of time:

first when the system of cymorth, mutual help
precluded the need for a Poor Rate
in the unbroken tradition of the farming hamlet
its innocence broken by copper

then through the mining boom
when a sympathetic priest
petitioned for the injured
to the agent of Lord Anglesey

and through the simultaneous trough of the wave:
a hut full of naked children
destitute of all conveniences
and almost all necessities.

a patchwork of rags to be coveted
under the threat of the red cloth badge
of dependence on the parish –
beginnings of the red menace in Wales:

in the wake of those years,
the visiting of the people
with a winter of cholera.

in the good times, neighbourly
hogs rooted at liberty in the streets.

now we have tourism, all the neat squares
the Tourist Board has sewn up most craftily.

Patchworks of Amlwch,
a pattern of fields and buildings
interlocking with lives.

Steve Griffiths

People:

Branwen

In The Mabinogion, *a collection of twelve medieval tales and a work unique in Welsh literature, Branwen, the daughter of Bendigeidfran, king of Britain, enters into marriage with Matholwch, the king of Ireland, in a symbolic act of unity between the two countries. But the marriage has the reverse effect and unleashes revenge and bloody violence.*

The marriage took place at Aberffraw, where this extract opens.

And they fixed upon Aberffraw as the place where she should become his bride. And they went thence, and towards Aberffraw the hosts proceeded; Matholwch and his host in their ships; Bendigeid Vran and his host by land, until they came to Aberffraw. And at Aberffraw they began the feast and sat down. And thus sat they. The King of the Island of the Mighty and Manawyddan the son of Llyr, on one side, and Matholwch on the other side, and Branwen the daughter of Llyr beside him. And they were not within a house, but under tents. No house could ever contain Bendigeid Vran. And they began the banquet and caroused and discoursed. And when it was more pleasing to them to sleep than to carouse, they went to rest, and that night Branwen became Matholwch's bride.

And next day they arose, and all they of the Court, and the officers began to equip and to range the horses and the attendants, and they ranged them in order as far as the sea.

And behold one day, Evnissyen, the quarrelsome man of whom it is spoken above, came by chance into the place, where the horses of Matholwch were, and asked whose horses they might be. 'They are the horses of Matholwch, king of Ireland, who is married to Branwen, thy sister; his horses are they.' 'And is it thus they have done with a maiden such as she, and moreover my sister, bestowing her without my consent? They could have offered no greater insult to me than this,' said he. And thereupon he rushed under the horses and cut off their lips at the teeth, and their ears close to their heads, and their tails close to their backs, and wherever he could clutch their eyelids, he cut them to the very bone, and he disfigured the horses and rendered them useless.

And they came with these tidings unto Matholwch, saying that the horses were disfigured, and injured so that not one of them could ever be of any use again. 'Verily, lord,' said one, 'it was an insult unto thee, and as such was it meant.' 'Of a truth, it is a marvel to me, that if they desire

102

to insult me, they should have given me a maiden of such high rank and so much beloved of her kindred, as they have done.' 'Lord,' said another, 'thou seest that thus it is, and there is nothing for thee to do but to go to thy ships.' And thereupon towards his ships he set out.

And tidings came to Bendigeid Vran that Matholwch was quitting the Court without asking leave, and messengers were sent to inquire of him wherefore he did so. And the messengers that went were Iddic the son of Anarawd, and Heveydd Hir. And these overtook him and asked of him what he designed to do, and wherefore he went forth. 'Of a truth,' said he, 'if I had known I had not come hither. I have been altogether insulted, no one had ever worse treatment than I have had here. But one thing surprises me above all.' 'What is that?' asked they. 'That Branwen the daughter of Llyr, one of the three chief ladies of this island, and the daughter of the King of the Island of the Mighty, should have been given me as my bride, and that after that I should have been insulted; and I marvel that the insult was not done me before they had bestowed upon me a maiden so exalted as she.' 'Truly, lord, it was not the will of any that are of the Court,' said they, 'nor of any that are of the council, that thou shouldest have received this insult; and as thou hast been insulted, the dishonour is greater unto Bendigeid Vran than unto thee.' 'Verily,' said he, 'I think so. Nevertheless he cannot recall the insult.' These men returned with that answer to the place where Bendigeid Vran was, and they told him what reply Matholwch had given them. 'Truly,' said he, 'there are no means by which we may prevent his going away at enmity with us, that we will not take.' 'Well, lord,' said they, 'send after him another embassy.' 'I will do so,' said he. 'Arise, Manawyddan son of Llyr, and Heveydd Hir, and Unic Glew Ysgwyd, and go after him, and tell him that he shall have a sound horse for every one that has been injured. And beside that, as an atonement for the insult, he shall have a staff of silver, as large and as tall as himself, and a plate of gold of the breadth of his face, and show unto him who it was that did this, and that it was done against my will; but that he who did it is my brother, by the mother's side, and therefore it would be hard for me to put him to death. And let him come and meet me,' said he, 'and we will make peace in any way he may desire.'

The embassy went after Matholwch, and told him all these sayings in a friendly manner, and he listened there-unto. 'Men,' said he, 'I will take counsel.' So to the council he went. And in the council they considered that if they should refuse this, they were likely to have more shame rather than to obtain so great an atonement. They resolved therefore to accept it, and they returned to the Court in peace.

Branwen died on the banks of Afon Alaw in a state of great sorrow for what she regarded as her part in the division between Britain and Ireland.

Branwen looked towards Ireland and towards the Island of the Mighty, to see if she could descry them. 'Alas,' said she, 'woe is me that I was ever born; two islands have been destroyed because of me!' Then she uttered a loud groan, and there broke her heart. And they made her a foursided grave, and buried her upon the banks of the Alaw.

The Mabinogion, translated by Charlotte Guest

Praise of Tudur Fychan's Sons

I am going to the land of Môn yonder,
often have I desired it,
to get to know the sons
of Tudur, chief jousters of Môn:
Gronwy, Rhys, lords of the island,
Ednyfed, Gwilym, keen spear;
Rhys, Ednyfed, gift-bestowing lord,
grim and keen his spear, Gwilym, Gronwy;
Ednyfed, Gronwy, Rhun's pride,
Rhys, Gwilym, splendour like that of Alun,
Gwilym, Gronwy, our lord,
Ednyfed, he gave a gift, mighty Rhys;
four great Nudds to me,
let Peter protect them, may it be at a good hour,
four sons – who insults them? –
children who will not let me be humbled,
solid as squares, four bright
evangelists by the sea of Môn,
prime oxen of Gwynedd, language of eulogy,
four yoked together in giving;
cubs of fierce Tudur Llwyd,
supporters of two hundred hearths,
giants of wine – it's easy to love the hawks –
magnificent stags, gentle hawks,
pillar shafts, chancellors,
columns of the edges of Môn,
fine magnanimous princes –
I am blessed – wine is their nourishment,

barons without fear,
proud plants of the front line,
descendants of Rhirid, eagles' flight,
the Wolf – not a man of churlish renown –
bulls of battle, bloody host,
augers of war, relentless in conflict,
children of Tudur, he was my eagle,
noble peacocks of a patriarch;
the host is armour on the sea-flood,
the foremost children are a golden litter.

I will go to Môn, I desire a gift,
sweet fair mountain land,
mother of Gwynedd, there I have
friends who are well-honoured in their locality;
fine monastery with a loverly border,
it is a cloister to me by an inlet of the sea,
a snug enclosure to nurture poets
without refusing anyone who would be nurtured.

The first place I will go, a lion who gives,
fortress of Penmon, stag of Penmynydd,
the house, I saw the fine fair place before,
of Tudur Llwyd, good is the place;
there is there, with no limit to gifts,
a re-creation of the hearth of Rheged,
Gronwy of the shining spear, pleasant court,
very good renown, no unpleasant man;
I will carry for my golden hawk
a spear and a banner, proud baron,
and a shield, chieftain's body,
with him to protect his body,
to fair Môn, no need to fear any man
with Iolo following him.

To Erddreiniog, it ennobled the island,
I will go, I will feast, to Rhys;
I am treasurer – I will seize his silver
and his burnished gold, a hundred know him –
to Rhys and his receiver
and his true friend – oh what a man!

By a fine song I will claim
all the wealth of his country.

Tre'rcastell is not far off, chamber of gifts,
heavenly land, Ednyfed's dwelling;
I will be his cup-bearer there
and his steward always – he is my gold;
I will get, without any better visit,
as good as him in Tre'rcastell.

Backwards and forwards to the border
I will go to Rhys, true summons;
across Môn from Rhys's house then,
fearlessly, to Gronwy's house;
from Gronwy's house, the good of the island,
I must return to Rhys's house;
from Rhys's house, steel his shield,
to the house of fine Gwilym, there will be great profit;
Gwilym's court, a mansion full of herbs,
golden leopard, place of ready talent,
dragon's nature, there will I dwell
in heaven, and I will do right,
Clorach's dwelling, brilliant building,
I will tarry in Môn as long as I live.

Iolo Goch: translated by Professor Dafydd Johnson

Never Without Song

My mind was very much excited: I was in the birth-place of the mighty
Tudors – I had just seen the tomb of one of them; I was also in the land of
the bard; a country which had produced Gwalchmai, who sang the
triumphs of Owain, and him who had sung the Cowydd of Judgment,
Gronwy Owen. So no wonder I was excited. On I went reciting bardic
snatches connected with Anglesey. At length I began repeating Black
Robin's ode in praise of the island, or rather my own translation of it,
executed more than thirty years before, which, amongst others, contains
the following lines:

'Twelve sober men the muses woo,
    Twelve sober men in Anglesey,
Dwelling at home, like patriots true,
    In reverence for Anglesey.'

'Oh,' said I, after I had recited that stanza, 'what would I not give to see one of those sober patriotic bards, or at least one of their legitimate successors, for by this time no doubt, the sober poets, mentioned by Black Robin, are dead. That they left legitimate successors who can doubt? for Anglesey is never to be without bards. Have we not the words, not of Robin the Black, but Huw the Red to that effect?

'Brodir, gnawd ynddi prydydd;
Heb ganu ni bu ni bydd.'

That is: a hospitable country, in which a poet is a thing of course. It has never been and will never be without song.'

George Borrow: 'Wild Wales' (1862)

Huw Owen was a recusant who refused to comply with accepted religious doctrine. After experiencing persecution he was engaged by Henry Somerset, the Lord Herbert, in London. Later he served Somerset as estate manager at Raglan Castle. He died at his home in Tintern, and in the world of scholarship is usually remembered nowadays for his Welsh translation of Thomas â Kempis' Imitation of Christ.

Huw Owen, Gwenynog, Anglesey
(1575-1642)

The *fistula in ano*
was what brought him to his Christ:
the fester of doubt,
the filth of an age
that looked at heaven
through the needle's eye.
A viper generation
that stripped the Christian saints,
and clothed Mammon
in their garments.
They peopled the shattered choirs,
the elegant monasteries,
with their numberless greedy hands,

made a squire of the poor priest,
and fed him on God's fatness.

For half a century
Huw Gwenynog
was satisfied with the old order.
He attended the Mass-less Sundays,
won peasants' respect,
and showed it in turn
to the new gentry
which polished its way to London
with the spit of arse-licking.
He disciplined the men of the *trained band*
to guard against the enemy across the water,
and he hated the name of Spain.

But his pain proved too much for him,
and he heeded the voice
of the despised remnant
who in their longing remained true
to the Old Faith.
'Go to Saint Cybi's waters,' they told him,
'and you will find relief.'

And he found it,
whether by miracle or accident,
who knows?

But the rest of his days
was a stripping away:
he lost his home,
his old haunts, his respect,
his family, his field-head.
He became an exile in his own land,
a refugee in its border-country.

But his faith never weakened:
he was sustained
by that which had been lost,
by a bareness and simplicity
that were in themselves

a form of stripping away.
The wafer
became a transparent glass
through which
he caught a glimpse of God.

Gareth Alban Davies: translated by the poet

A Curse on Holyhead

Lo here I sit at holy head
With muddy ale and mouldy bread
All Christian victuals stink of fish
I'm where my enemies would wish
Convict of lies is every sign,
The Inn has not one drop of wine
I'm fastened both by wind and tide
I see the ship at anchor ride
The Captain swears the sea's too rough
He has not passengers enough.
And thus the Dean is forced to stay
Till others come to help the pay
In Dublin they'd be glad to see
A packet though it brings in me.
They cannot say the winds are cross
Your Politicians at a loss
For want of matter swears and frets,
Are forced to read the old gazettes.
I never was in haste before
To reach that slavish hateful shore
Before, I always found the wind
To me was most malicious kind
But now, the danger of a friend
On whom my fears and hopes depend
Absent from whom all Climes are cursed
With whom I'm happy in the worst
With rage impatient makes me wait
A passage to the land I hate.
Else, rather on this bleaky shore
Where loudest winds incessant roar

Where neither herb nor tree will thrive,
I'd go in freedom to my grave,
Than Rule yon Isle and be a Slave.

Jonathan Swift: 'Holyhead Journal' (1727)

Editor's Note: According to Lord Orrany, a contemporary, Swift relished low life.

'He generally chose to dine with waggoners, ostlers and persons of that rank; and he used to lye at night in houses where he found written over the door 'Lodgings for a Penny'. He delighted in scenes of low life. The vulgar dialect was not only a fount of humour for him, but I verily believed was acceptable to his nature . . . '

The Further Grumbles of Swift

April 2nd, 1735. One o'clock in the evening had notice of the *Prince Frederick* Packet being to go over that evening; took a coach half an hour past two in the evening; came to George's Quay, paid 1s. for a small bowl of Punch, took water at 4, and came on board the Packet Boat, taking leave of my good friend and Cousin William Parry on the Quay (Having left his daughter in Dublin).

April 3rd. The wind E.S.E.; weighed anchor at 4 in the morning; sailed all that day against the wind; made very little way, being not above 7 leagues from the Irish shore by night, the wind continuing E., fair, but he says it is too fierce; I believe he wants more company.' The 26th: 'The weather is fiercer and wilder than yesterday, yet the Captain now dreams of sailing . . . I should be glad to talk with Farmers and Shopkeepers but none of them speak English. A Dog is better company than the Vicar, for I remember him of old . . . The Master of the packet-boat, one Jones, hath not treated me with the least civility, although Watt gave him my name. In short I come from being used like an Emperor to be used worse than a Dog at Holyhead. Yet my hat is worn to pieces by answering the civilities of the poor inhabitants as they pass by.' The 28th: 'Tis allowed that we learn patience by suffering. I have not spirit enough left me to fret . . . Well it is now three in the afternoon. I have dined and revisited the Master; the wind and tide serve, and I am just taking boat to go to the ship.' The 29th, Friday: 'You will now know something of what it is to be at sea. We had not been half an hour in the ship till a fierce wind rose directly against us; we tried a good while, but the storm still continued, so we turned back and it was 8 at night, dark and raining, before the ship got back at anchor. The other passengers went back in a boat to Holyhead, but to prevent accidents and broken shins I lay all night on board and came back this morning at 8. Am now in my chamber, where I must stay and get a fresh stock of patience.'

Jonathan Swift (1647-1745): 'Holyhead Journal; (1727)

A Feeling of Disgust

On arriving at Holyhead, I chose to go to Mr Moran's Hotel, where we immediately deposited our coats and luggage, and ordered breakfast. But while this was preparing, we followed, and mixed with the long and motley train that were hastening to the pier, where we witnessed the embarkation of the mail bags and passengers, on board Captain Powers' steam-packet, for Ireland. This was a gratification of a novel kind. Captain P. himself afforded us some amusement. That gentleman had the appearance of a right merry fellow when he pleased, but never without recollections of office. His air was authoritative, his voice loud and quick, and his orders were obeyed on board and ashore, as though they were the fiat of destiny. He moved his chapeau to all strangers who were well-dressed, and familiarly shook hands with old acquaintance. Exactly at half past six, he sung out, with watch in hand, 'Is all a-board?' and receiving affirmative reply, he ordered the vessel to be shoved off. Three of the hands immediately stepped forward, and applying their arms and bodies to the masonry of the pier, the packet was disengaged, and the steam-engine being set in motion, the vessel darted forward with rapidity, and soon cleared the pier head. Its movement struck me as harsh lines in a picture would do. I revolted from it as unnatural; but this was only because I was unaccustomed to it. With all its celerity of motion, there yet seemed a vast labour in the perpetual beating of the water, by the paddles of the engine; and her noise, and the stream of black smoke that came from her chimney, increased my feeling of disgust.

G. Freeman: 'Sketches in Wales' (1826)

Grace Parry

. . . the ensuing day we crossed the Menai in order to visit Anglesey. Several ferries ply on this trajectus. We fortunately took that of Garth-Point, about half a mile from Bangor, which afforded us a very curious and singular character. It is worked by an old woman, by name Grace Parry, but more commonly called, from the place of her abode, Gras-y-Garth; a short, thick, squat female, who, though upwards of sixty winters have passed over her head, is as strong as a horse, and as active as one of her own country goats. Her excellence in rowing and managing a boat is unrivalled through the coast, but cannot be wondered at, as she served an early apprenticeship to the business, under her father and mother, who lived at the same little cottage which she inhabits, and worked the same passage for the better part of the past century. The prowess of her mother, and the skill of her father, are still the favourite themes of her discourse. She remembers with particular pleasure his ability in *swimming*, (for he seems to have been nearly an amphibious animal) and, as a proof of it, relates a circumstance that frequently occurred, even when he had passed his grand climacterick. The ferry was generally plied by the joint exertions of this couple, who, upon the whole, were tolerably *loving*; but as storms will happen in the fairest days, so their conjugal serenity was occasionally disturbed; and sometimes an altercation would take place when they were ferrying their passengers across the Menai. In these cases, the wife, who was the *better man* of the two, so compleatly worsted her spouse in obloquy and abuse, that, unable to bear it, he would suddenly cast off his jacket, leap into the Menai, and swim towards his cottage, bidding his dame, with a string of Welsh execrations, take care of the passengers herself. Nothing initimidates this Cambrian heroine; she stands in fear of no human being, and is equally regardless of the rage of the elements. Last winter her *boat* drifted away in the night, and Grace for some days thought it had been stove to pieces. However, as it was her *free-hold estate*, she made diligent enquiry after it, and at length discovered that it had been taken up and carried to Liverpool. Engaging a stout fellow in the neighbourhood to accompany her, she instantly set off for this port on foot, though nearly sixty miles distant, and having recovered her property, embarked on board the skiff, (not more than twelve or thirteen feet on the keel) and with the assistance of her companion, actually rowed it back to Garth-Point, through heavy seas and squally weather, as perilous a voyage as ever was performed.

As we found Grace's prejudices against the English were rather violent, and not knowing to what length they might carry her, particularly when she was under the influence of *cwrrw da*, we thought it necessary, for the safety of future Saxon travellers, to reward her labours with double the sum she demanded. This unexpected generosity so gratified the old woman, that she swore most bitterly we were the *greatest gentlemen* she ever met with; she declared, she should always like the

English for our sake, and insisted upon shaking hands with us individually at parting. We indulged her wish, but (whether she meant it as a token of her kindness, or a proof of her strength, I know not) gave us each such a serious *grip* as almost dislocated our fingers.

Richard Warner: 'A Second Walk Through Wales' (1798)

A Literary Pilgrimage

When I started from Bangor, to visit the birth-place of Gronwy Owen, I by no means saw my way clearly before me. I knew that he was born in Anglesey in a parish called Llanfair Mathafarn Eithaf, that is St Mary's of farther Mathafarn – but as to where this Mathafarn lay, north or south, near or far, I knew positively nothing. Passing through the northern suburb of Bangor I saw a small house in front of which was written 'post-office' in white letters; before this house underneath a shrub in a little garden sat an old man reading. Thinking that from this person, whom I judged to be the post-master, I was as likely to obtain information with respect to the place of my destination as from anyone, I stopped and taking off my hat for a moment, inquired whether he could tell me anything about the direction of a place called Llanfair Mathafarn Eithaf. He did not seem to understand my question, for getting up he came towards me and asked what I wanted: I repeated what I had said, whereupon his face became animated.

'Llanfair Mathafarn Eithaf!' said he. 'Yes, I can tell you about it, and with good reason, for it lies not far from the place where I was born.'

The above was the substance of what he said, and nothing more, for he spoke in English somewhat broken.

'And how far is Llanfair from here?' said I.

'About ten miles,' he replied.

'That's nothing,' said I; 'I was afraid it was much farther.'

'Do you call ten miles nothing,' said he, 'in a burning day like this? I think you will be both tired and thirsty before you get to Llanfair, supposing you go there on foot. But what may your business be at Llanfair?' said he, looking at me inquisitively.

'It is a strange place to go to, unless you go to buy hogs or cattle.'

'I go to buy neither hogs nor cattle,' said I, 'though I am somewhat of a judge of both; I go on a more important errand, namely to see the birth-place of the great Gronwy Owen.'

'Are you any relation of Gronwy Owen?' said the old man, looking at me more inquisitively than before, through a large pair of spectacles, which he wore.

'None whatever,' said I.

'Then why do you go to see his parish? it is a very poor one.'

'From respect to his genius,' said I; 'I read his works long ago, and was delighted with them.'

'Are you a Welshman?' said the old man.

'No,' said I, 'I am no Welshman.'

'Can you speak Welsh?' said he, addressing me in that language.

'A little,' said I; 'but not so well as I can read it.'

'Well,' said the old man, 'I have lived here a great many years, but never before did a Saxon call upon me, asking questions about Gronwy Owen or his birth-place. Immortality to memory! I owe much to him, for reading his writings taught me to be a poet!'

'Dear me!' said I, 'are you a poet?'

'I trust I am,' said he; 'though the humblest of Ynys Fon.'

A flash of proud fire, methought, illumined his features as he pronounced these last words.

'I am most happy to have met you,' said I; 'but tell me how am I to get to Llanfair?'

'You must go first,' said he, 'to Traeth Coch, which in Saxon is called the 'Red Sand.' In the village called the Pentraeth which lies above that sand, I was born; through the village and over the bridge you must pass, and after walking four miles due north you will find yourself in Llanfair Eithaf, at the northern extremity of Mon. Farewell! That ever Saxon should ask me about Gronwy Owen, and his birth-place! I scarcely believe you to be a Saxon, but whether you be or not, I repeat farewell.'

George Borrow: 'Wild Wales' (1862)

Goronwy Owen

The life of this unfortunate and expatriated son of genius, is so complicated, and so very painful in the detail, that I would willingly draw a veil over the pages that recite nothing but poverty and distresses, which he had to contend with from the first dawn of his youth, for Goronwy Owen the acknowledged 'chief bard among the modern poets of Cymru,' went to school by stealth, his father beating him for it, unless his mother was by to prevent him. In 1745, he was ordained to a curacy, in Mona, i.e. Llanvair-yn-mathavarn, the parish in which he had been born; out of this he was soon ousted by the bishop's chaplain, who wanted 'a title for his friend Mr John Ellis.' He was obliged to go and serve a church, near Oswestry, where he married in 1747, a person whose family were reputed affluent, but says Mr Owen, 'I have never been the better for them.' This was written in a letter to Lewis Morris, his first patron, about the year 1750, in which he says, 'Pray look out for a situation for me in Wales: I care not a rush in what part, for here I am serving the curacy of Uppington, and together with a school, is only £26 a year, and what is that to keep a wife and two boys, especially in England, where everything is so dear.' In 1755, he was curate of Northolt, in the same county of Salop. Worn out with unavailing expectations of obtaining some small preferment in his native country, he, in 1757, addressed a letter to the Cymrydorion Society, praying for some small allowance towards paying the passage of himself and family to America, 'and thus' (observes his feeling biographer and brother bard, the amiable Dr Owen Pugh,) 'was the fairest flower of British genius, transplanted to wither in the ungenial climes of America.' In 1767, he sent over an elegy on the death of his earliest and true friend, who first found out his abilities, Lewis Morris; this was the last account which ever came from himself, and when in 1793, some gentlemen who revered the memory of Goronwy Owen, tried to obtain information respecting the time he died, &c. with a view of setting up a monument, 'sent letters to his son, him they found perfectly Americanized.'

Goronwy Owen wrote *Cywydd y Farn*, which is considered one of the best poetical compositions in the Cambro-British language; he also translated several of the Odes of Horace, in all their native force and humour, into Welsh, so pure and classical as to defy criticism, and (unlike some of our modern learned) so plain as to be 'intelligible to the meanest capacity.'

Angharad Llwyd: 'A History of the Island of Mona' (1833)

The Invitation

(sent from Northolt, in the year 1745, to William Parry,
Deputy Comptroller of the Mint)

Parry, of all my friends the best,
Thou who thy Maker cherishest,
Thou who regard'st me so sincere,
And who to me art no less dear;
Kind friend, in London since thou art,
To love thee's not my wisest part;

This separation's hard to bear:
To love thee not far better were.

But wilt thou not from London town
Journey some day to Northolt down,
Song to obtain, O sweet reward,
And walk the garden of the Bard? –
But thy employ, the year throughout,
In wandering the White Tower about,
Moulding and stamping coin with care,
The farthing small and shilling fair.
Let for a month thy Mint lie still,
Covetous be not, little Will;
Fly from the birth-place of the smoke,
Nor in that wicked city choke;
O come, though money's charms be strong,
And if thou come I'll give thee song,
A draught of water, hap what may,
Pure air to make thy spirits gay,
And welcome from an honest heart,
That's free from every guileful art.
I'll promise – fain thy face I'd see –
yet something more, sweet friend, to Thee:
The poet's *cwrw*[1] thou shalt prove,
In talk with him the garden rove,
Where in each leaf thou shalt behold
The Almighty's wonders manifold;
And every flower, in verity,
Shall unto thee show visibly,
In every fibre of its frame,
His deep design, who made the same. –
A thousand flowers stand here around,
With glorious brightness some are crown'd:
How beauteous art thou, lily fair!
With thee no silver can compare:
I'll not forget thy dress outshone
The pomp of regal Solomon.

I write the friend, I love so well,
No sounding verse his heart to swell.
The fragile flowerets of the plain

Can rival human triumphs vain.
I liken to a floweret's fate
The fleeting joys of mortal state;
The flower so glorious seen today
Tomorrow dying fades away:
An end has soon the flowery clan
And soon arrives the end of man;
The fairest floweret ever known
Would fade when cheerful summer's flown;
Then hither haste, ere turns the wheel!
Old age doth on these flowers steal;
Though pass'd two-thirds of autumn-time,
Of summer temperature's the clime;
The garden shows no sickliness,
The weather old age vanquishes,
The leaves are greenly glorious still –
But friend! grow old they must and will.

The rose, at edge of winter now,
Doth fade with all its summer glow;
Old are become the roses all,
Decline to age we also shall;
And with this prayer I'll end my lay,
Amen, with me, O Parry say;
To us be rest from all annoy,
And a robust old age of joy;
May we, ere pangs of death we know,
Back to our native Mona go;
May pleasant days us there await,
United and inseparate!
And the dread hour, when God shall please
To bid our mutual journey cease,
May Christ, who reigns in heaven above,
Receive us to his breast of love.

Goronwy Owen: translated by George Borrow

[1]*ale* (translator's note).

The Wish

Could I have what I begged for from heaven,
What I'd ask would be after this fashion,
Not an idle favour of fortune – no,
　　This upright choice would be my ambition:

Alert good sense, unpampered body,
To have from health a heart that's healthy,
And to leave then the unruly, officious
　　World, over-distressed and filthy.

I'd go back to my fathers' country,
Live respected, not lavish nor meagrely,
In sunlit Môn, a land most lovely, with
　　Cheerful men in it, full of ability.

A fair tithe, a parish that's orderly,
Home under hill, and books in plenty,
And a row of cattle in my diary, cared for
　　By the brisk wife Elin, fair and kindly.

For me, I'd wish for most, a garden,
A bower sheltered to suit the season,
Whilst I'd read the elegant diction of poets,
　　Seed of Druids, a deft recitation.

And over my head, amid the branches,
A paradise of sweet, pure voices,
Treble of finches, echoing verses, chirps
　　Of songful blithe birds' vowelled speeches.

And while the birds were at their singing,
Lest the bower incline me to sleeping,
Against the treble choir competing – my song,
　　Worthily versified, gay and diverting.

Myself, with my two boys around me,
I'd listen to Robyn rhymin gaily
To the apt strings of Goronwy – if two hands
    On the harp he'll learn to delight me.

Let the Englishman have what he's after,
A wild-running brookful of crystal water
Through some dear glen – he's welcome rather – if I
    Have Môn: for foremost I name her.

Grandiloquent she'll not make my praises,
Remembering gems, priceless prodigies,
Seas, land, mountain, leaf-laid copses, treasure
    Of far-off India's golden fringes.

The Pope loves Rome, a fine-built bastion;
Paris towers are gracious to Frenchmen;
The English has no need to mention London's
    Splendour of men: but Môn's my dear one.

A just return there, may God grant me,
And an unplagued age that will not irk me,
And children to cherish deftly their language,
    And a noble muse to give them glory!

Goronwy Owen: translated by Tony Conran

The Man in Grey

After we had all taken a full view of one another I said in Welsh, addressing myself to the man in grey, 'Pray may I take the liberty of asking the name of this place?'

'I believe you are an Englishman, sir,' said the man in grey, speaking English, 'I will therefore take the liberty of answering your question in the English tongue. The name of this place is Dyffryn Gaint.'

'Thank you,' said I; 'you are quite right with regard to my being an Englishman, perhaps you are one yourself?'

'Sir,' said the man in grey, 'I have not the honour to be so, I am a native of the small island, in which we are.'

'Small,' said I, 'but famous, particularly for producing illustrious men.'

'That's very true indeed, sir,' said the man in grey, drawing himself up; 'it is particularly famous for producing illustrious men.'

'There was Owen Tudor?' said I.

'Very true,' said the man in grey, 'his tomb is in the church a little way from hence.'

'Then,' said I, 'there was Gronwy Owen, one of the greatest bards that ever lived. Out of reverence to his genius I went yesterday to see the place of his birth.'

'Sir,' said the man in grey, 'I should be sorry to leave you without enjoying your conversation at some length. In yonder house they sell good ale, perhaps you will not be offended if I ask you to drink some with me and my friend?'

'You are very kind,' said I, 'I am fond of good ale, and fonder still of good company – suppose we go in?'

The ale, though not very good, was cool and neither sour nor bitter; we then sat for a moment or two in silence, my companions on one side of the table, and I on the other. After a little time the man in grey looking at me said:

'Travelling I suppoose in Anglesey for pleasure?'

'To a certain extent,' said I; 'but my chief object in visiting Anglesey was to view the birthplace of Gronwy Owen; I saw it yesterday and am now going to Holyhead chiefly with a view to seeing the country.'

'And how came you, an Englishman, to know anything of Gronwy Owen?'

'I studied Welsh literature when young,' said I, 'and was much struck with the verses of Gronwy: he was one of the great bards of Wales, and certainly the most illustrious genius that Anglesey ever produced.'

'A great genius I admit,' said the man in grey, 'but pardon me, not exactly the greatest Ynys Môn has produced. The race of the bards is not quite extinct in the island, sir. I could name one or two – however, I leave others to do so – but I assure you the race of bards is not quite extinct here.'

'I am delighted to hear you say so,' said I, 'and make no doubt that you speak correctly, for the Red Bard has said that Mona is never to be without a poet – but where am I to find one? Just before I saw you I was wishing to see a poet; I would willingly give a quart of ale to see a genuine Anglesey poet.'

'You would, sir, would you?' said the man in grey, lifting his head on high, and curling his upper lip.

'I would, indeed,' said I, 'my greatest desire at present is to see an Anglesey poet, but where am I to find one?'

'Where is he to find one?' said he of the tattered hat; 'where's the gwr boneddig to find a prydydd? No occasion to go far, he, he, he.'

'Well,' said I, 'but where is he?'

'Where is he? why there,' said he, pointing to the man in grey – 'the greatest prydydd in Ynys Môn or the whole world.'

George Borrow: 'Wild Wales' (1862)

The four renowned Morris brothers, had a wide ranging influence on life in eighteenth century Wales.

Although he spent much of his life in London, Richard sought to preserve the traditional songs of Ynys Môn and these give us an insight into the history of the region. William was employed as a Collector of Taxes at Holyhead and his interests lay both in the field of literature and botany. John died in Spain in a naval attack, but during his lifetime shared his brothers' interest in the cultural life of the island. The eldest of the brothers, Lewis, is probably the one who is best remembered today. The Carmarthenshire-born poet of the nineteenth century, Sir Lewis Morris, was a great-grandson of Lewis Morris of Ynys Môn and wrote a long poem in tribute to his four distinguished predecessors. Here are a few extracts from the poem, which is characterised by an attempt to write in the style of his contemporary, Tennyson.

From
On Four Patriot Brothers

All held their country dear, all prized as we
Her long heroic Past, her ancient tongue
That blossoms still, her strong sons' bravery,
Her songs, by lover and by warrior sung.

Here, through their own quaint use of either speech
We know them, now their native accents tell
Their story, now in nervous Saxon each
Brother to brother speaks, and both are well.

Here no unreal eulogy arrays
The dead in robes not theirs, nor partial hand
Conceals 'neath insincere or venal praise,
Foibles, it profits well to understand.

But each fraternal soul with loving care
Reveals itself; unchanged through time and change
And absence, still its inner thought lays bare
Nor thro' the estranging mists of years grows strange.

But frank and boyish still, can ne'er forget
'Mid service of the State and pride of place
The farm, the handicraft, and lingering yet –
The sire's shrewd wit, the mother's kindly grace.

Thus in close concord, lived they, till the call
Sounded too soon, which comes alike to all,
And severed here the gracious brotherhood
Knit fast by patriot aims and common blood.

Sir Lewis Morris (1896)

A Useful and Scientific Man

Alluding to the music of Wales, Lewis Morris says, 'The Druidical Bards knew how to sing, before Rome had a name, 'so never' (he continues) 'hereafter mention such moderns as Horace and Virgil, when you talk of

British poetry; Llywarch Hên, Taliesin, Aneurin, those followers of the druids, are our men, and nature our rule,' &c. This useful and scientific man, died at Penybryn, in the sixty-third year of his age, on the 11th. of April, 1765. Lewis Morris published under the Lords of the Admirality, Charts of the Coast, and Plans of the Harbours from Orme's Head to Milford Haven, from actual surveys made by himself, though he had no education, but what he acquired by his own genius and industry. These are by far the most correct charts of those coasts extant; he pointed out the very spot, subsequently chosen by Rennie for the pier, at Holyhead. Had the latter followed more closely the directions pointed out by this clear-headed native, the harbour would have been less liable to the dreadfully frequent catastrophe of shipwreck, owing to its too narrow entrance.

Angharad Llwyd: 'A History of the Island of Mona' (1833)

The Morris Letters

The Morris brothers corresponded with each other regularly, and their letters reveal much about both their lives and personalities and the age in which they lived.

A Londoner of whom Gronwy (Owen) had bought house-hold stuff to a considerable value, went to him the other day for his money, and a writ in his pocket to take his body if he did not deliver him back the goods and a watch, etc. But Gronwy (like a) valiant Briton, on sight of him bristled up, and rattled him, and told him he had no business to trouble *him* or to come so far, that he was not to be used in that manner. But the man told him: 'I have a writ in my pocket and an officer here to execute it, and if you don't deliver me my goods by fair means I shall make bold with your body and carry it to yᵉ county gaol which is Newgate. Give me that watch first of all,' says the tyrant. The ancient Britain's courage failing him, put his hands in his fob and took out yᵉ watch and deliverd it, but first he took off a silk string that was to it, (value 2d.) and then put up the affront. The Briton insisted that he was of a good family and a very ancient nation, and it was not right to strip him of all, for he had no bed to lie on, and after abusing his tyranical creditor to some purpose, he got off clear for that time at the expense of the watch which he had never paid for, nor ever intended to pay for it, nor ever will pay for any thing if he can help it, for I believe he thinks all mankind obliged to find him all necessaries. Is not he poet for the nation of yᵉ Britains?

Letter from Lewis Morris to William Morris
October 16th 1756

Dear Brother, – I sent yesterday a letter to you to the Post Office, but this comes on a sudden emergency not foreseen. Molly Lewis (Mrs Hicks' daughter) came here last night from Gallt Vadog, bewailing and crying that her mother is at the point of death. She had been afflicted this good while with a violent overflowing . . . or perhaps some vessels bursting, and all remedies tried but to no purpose; for two days ago, the flux broke out afresh, more violent than ever, upon some visitors telling her that her husband was very ill, they not daring to tell her of his death, for that would have knocked her up directly. There is the greatest probability in the world that she can live but a few days, and these poor women, her daughters, are in such distress that they have not the wherewithal to bury her. Molly came from Warwickshire (where her husband lives), in order to lye in at her mother's, and expects herself to be brought to bed every minute, and her chief dependance was on her mother. Nelly, the other sister, is far out of order and almost blind. They have both joined in a letter to-day to Mr Wise, the hatter, to desire him to remit them £8 or £10 for their mother's use, of the money Mr Hicks had in his bureau (about £30 I think), and to pay it into your hands, giving a receipt to Mr Wise for Widdow Hicks's use. And as soon as you give me an account of it I'll pay it here. It is not convenient for me to pay more than £10 at present. They have received letters from Mr Wise and Charles Griffiths, giving an account of Mortimer Hicks's death, with an inventory of his effects, but they have not ventured to give their mother the least hint of them, and it seems to me there is no probability of her recovering, for she has not spoke to anybody this two days, and is in a dozing sleep all the while . . . it is a miserable condition of these poor women are in, poorer than any beggar that goes about for bread, for their spirits cannot stoop to beg.

I am, your affectionate brother, Lewis Morris.

Letter to Richard Morris June 24th, 1760

A bold stroke was made at the Surveyor and myself the other day. A busy fellow of this place, a taylor by trade, was made a boatman about some three years ago, who, presuming upon his interest with Sir Nicholas Baily, whose voter he is, and eggd on by a discarded officer, one Hugh Lloyd, complained first to the Salt Board and lately to the Surveyor General of certain pretended crimes we were guilty of. We had, last week and this, an examination, when all appeared to the surveyor General, to be but a malicious scheme. What makes me be somewhat particular in this affair is, that I understand you are acquainted with Sir W. Irby. The first of these chaps, viz., Robert Griffith, holds a lease under Sir William, and the latter (H. Lloyd) is a tennant of his in this place. He is a fellow that made himself infamous by his tricks; was formerly collector of this place, but turned for defrauding the King, as he was out of the Salts and out of being Coastwaiter of the Customs a second time. This was the chief person concerned in the scheme of Thomas Jones against brother Lewis, where a set of villains joind to ruin him, but were repulsed with shame and infamy. He has the best bargain in the county under Sir William. A large inn, with abundance of out-houses, barn, stable, a fine field well waterd, garden, etc., and all for £10 per annum! Gresyn na byddai fodd i wneuthur ir hen leidr gymwynas, am ei ddrwg weithredodd. The other fellow (rhyngwy i a chwitheu) I believe will be out. If Sir Nicholas won't intermeddle (I wish Sir William mayn't), for he is not capable of the duty, and is disobedient and insolent. None but a villain of the blackest dye would have offered to hurt such a person as the Surveyor, who has a housefull of small children and nothing but his business to maintain 'em. He is a sober, diligent, careful man, and perhaps discharges his duty as well as any officer in the Revenue.

Letter from William Morris to Richard Morris from Caergybi
August 12th 1757

Bone Setters

These men and women were of humble origin and their fame was largely confined to their island community but they were the ancestors of one who was to become a part of surgical history and who is rightly described as the father of modern orthopaedic surgery. He was a man who pioneered in the wilderness and who did not live to see his principles accepted by the medical profession but his teaching has brought immeasurable relief to suffering humanity.

The origin of the family is clouded in mystery and whether the accepted version is fact or fiction, truth or legend is debatable. What is known for certain is that there lived a man in the parish of Llanfairynghornwy, on the north west coast of Anglesey, during the years 1745-1814, who was to become the first of a long line of descendants with the inherent gift of bone-setting. It is who he was and whence he came that remains an enigma.

A well known smuggler, Dannie Lukie, practised his nefarious activities along the stretch of coast between Cemaes and Holyhead and it is said that one dark and stormy night, whilst trying to locate a vessel to receive his illegal goods, he eventually found it sinking and nearby a drifting boat with two small boys clinging to its sides. He succeeded in rescuing them but one of them died a short time afterwards. The other was adopted and brought up by a Dr Lloyd, who lived at nearby Mynachdy. Even this is open to doubt for some believe that it was at Maes, Llanfairynghornwy that he found a home, but I consider it more likely that his later gifts of healing would more readily have developed under the guidance of a medical man rather than of the farmer living at Maes. The fact that this house became his home in later years is a possible cause for the doubt that exists.

He was given, we are told, the name of Thomas because he was a twin. His first name was Evan. Controversy abounds about his nationality. The most commonly accepted belief is that he was Spanish but there are some who argue that he was of Scottish stock and others that he originated in the Isle of Man. The most widely held view favours Spanish ancestry. Mr H. Hughes-Roberts, whose careful research of the family resulted in his excellent book *Meddygon Esgyrn Môn* and to whom I am indebted for much of my information, corresponded with the Spanish Embassy in London. He had been able to furnish them with the predominant features of Evan Thomas's appearance – a man of small stature, strong and muscular, jet black hair and blue eyes and of dignified presence – and in reply they wrote:

> I am aware that the practice of bonesetting prevails, particularly in the Celtic regions; that is to say, Galicia and Asturias and the Celtic-Iberian part of Castile.
>
> The person to whom you refer is typical, not of Spaniards generally, but of a kind of Celtic Spaniard living in some parts of Asturias, Galicia and Castile.

The suggestion that he was of Scottish descent arose out of the fact that the date of the shipwreck corresponded with the time of the Jacobite rebellion and that the ship may have been smuggling arms from Scotland to Anglesey. There is no evidence to support this contention and even less for the Isle of Man suggestion. This is based purely on the fact that at one time smuggling between the two islands was rife. No one will know with certainty where the first Evan Thomas originated, but what is beyond doubt is that he must be the starting point of the narrative of the Anglesey bonesetters.

W. Hywel Jones in the Transactions of the Anglesey Antiquarian Society Transactions (1981)

John Wesley and Captain Griffiths

Mr Wesley passed through Anglesey to Ireland on several occasions, and was compelled to spend considerable time in the neighbourhood of Holyhead. The old sailing boats, without the business competition of the present day, were too slow for the founder of Methodism. On his first visit nothing special is recorded, which was on August 7, 1747. Returning from Ireland he called at Rhydyspardyn, which was then occupied by Thomas Thomas. The family not knowing English, Mr Wesley, to his delight, was welcomed to the house of Mr Morgan, a schoolmaster. In the month of February, on Wednesday the 24th, 1748, he came to Holyhead, and found all the ships on the other side, and in consequence he was delayed in the neighbourhood till the 8th March. On the Thursday and Friday evenings he preached in a room, which was crowded with decent and well-behaved people. On the second night the clergyman was rather agitated, and in a threatening attitude. Mr Swindells, Mr Welsey's companion, accompanied the minister to his lodgings, and the two had a friendly conversation. The clergyman's trouble was caused by the people leaving the church, and at Mr Swindells's suggestion Mr Wesley wrote *A Word to a Methodist*, which Mr Ellis translated into Welsh. On the Sunday, Monday and Tuesday evenings, Mr Wesley preached to large congregations. The delay, however, was causing him considerable inconvenience, and the lame excuses made by the captains for not sailing created some annoyance, which he said put him in mind of an epigram –

'There are, if rightly I methink,
Five causes why a man should drink,'

which, slightly altered, would just suit the occasion –

'There are, unless my memory fail,
Five causes why we should not sail:
The fog is thick, the wind is high,
It rains, or may do by and by,
Or any other reason why.'

He called to see a Mr Jones, an acquaintance of his brother, with a Mr Holloway, an exciseman, who resolved to set out afresh. The frivolity of this man's wife had been a great hindrance to him, but she had been deeply wrought upon by a series of dreams and a flash of lightning, and both husband and wife appeared to be anxious about their souls.

Mr Wesley accepted the hospitality of Mr Holloway, the exciseman, who was residing in a little, quiet, solitary spot, a retreat he most heartily desired, where no human voice was heard but that of the family. On the following Wednesday evening Mr Wesley preached to a large congregation who were willing to hear, and at about eleven they went on board. It was a dark night, with much rain and high wind. When Mr Wesley and Mr Christopher Hopper retired from the deck, there was on the deck a Captain Griffiths of Carnarvonshire, whom Mr Wesley describes as a clumsy, overgrown, hard-faced man, whose countenance resembled that of one of the ruffians in 'Macbeth', which he had seen some thirty years before at Drury Lane. As Mr Wesley was about to lie down, this man tumbled in, and he poured out such a volléy of ribaldry, obscenity, and blasphemy, every second or third word being an oath, as was scarce ever heard at Billingsgate. The boat was driven back by the storm, and they were obliged to wait on shore for a whole week before they could sail again for Dublin. Captain Griffiths, with a number of men, maddened with intoxicating drink, burst open the door of the house where Mr Wesley was staying, struck old Robert Griffith the landlord, kicked his wife, and demanded the parson. The landlord slipped away quietly, removed Mr Wesley to a more private room, and locked him in. The enraged captain followed, and broke open one or two doors, and while on a chair, looking on the top of the bed, he fell, hurt himself badly, and after a while with his troop walked away. Mr Wesley went down and spent half an hour in prayer with a company of poor people. About nine o'clock, just when the family were preparing for bed, the house was beset again, the mad captain burst open the door, and was soon in the passage. Robert Griffith's daughter had a pail of water, and whether intentionally or from fright, she immersed the captain from head to foot. He cried as well as he could, 'Murder! murder!' and stood still for a few moments. In the meantime Robert Griffith stepped by him and locked the door. He had thus lost his companians, and began to change the tone of his voice, and shouted, 'Let me out! let me out!' After giving his word of honour not to interfere further, the door was opened, and he and his company went away.

David Young: 'The Origins and History of Methodism in Wales (1893)

'The Confusion of Tongues'

Sunday 6th March 1748: We went to Llangefni church, though we understood little of what we heard. Oh what a heavy curse was the Confusion of Tongues! And how grievous are the effects of it! All the birds of the air, all the beasts of the field, understand the language of their own species. Man only is a barbarian to man, unintelligible to his own brethren.

John Wesley: Journal (1747)

Christmas Evans

On his arrival in Anglesey he found ten small Baptist Societies, lukewarm and faint; what amount of life there was in them was spent in the distraction of theological controversy, which just then appeared to rage, strong and high, among the Baptists in North Wales. He was the only minister amongst those Churches, and he had not a brother minister to aid him within a hundred and fifty miles; but he commenced his labours in real earnest, and one of his first movements was to appoint a day of fasting and prayer in all the preaching places; he soon had the satisfaction to find a great revival, and it may with truth be said 'the pleasure of the Lord prospered in his hand.'

Llangefni appears to have been the spot in Anglesey where Christmas found his home. Llangefni is a respectable town now; when the preaching apostle arrived there, near a hundred years since, its few scattered houses did not even rise to the dignity of a village. Cildwrn Chapel was here the place of his ministrations, and here stood the little cottage where Christmas and his wife passed their plain and simple days. Chapel and cottage stood upon a bleak and exposed piece of ground. The cottage has been reconstructed since those days, but upon the site of the queer and quaint old manse stands now a far more commodious chapel-keeper's house. As in the Bedford vestry they show you still the chair in which John Bunyan sat, so here they show a venerable old chair, Christmas Evans's chair, in the old Cildwrn cottage; it is deeply and curiously marked by the cuttings of his pocket-knife, made when he was indulging in those reveries and day-dreams in the which he lived abstracted from everything around him.

Paxton Hood: 'Christmas Evans' (1904)

Men of Beaumaris

George Borrow does not relate any converations with local people at Beaumaris, but if he had he might have been told the remarkable story of William Lewis, who died at Beaumaris in 1793. Each morning of his life was devoted to the reading of portions of the scriptures and each evening to the consumption of as many as eight gallons of ale. When he died he weighed forty stone and it was necessary to elevate him out of his home with a specially constructed crane. He was evidently something of an eccentric for he dubbed himself 'the King of Spain'.

Eight years after Borrow's visit Richard Rowlands met a sad fate and was hanged at Beaumaris Gaol, having been accused of the murder of his father-in-law. He insisted that he was completely innocent and prior to his execution barricaded himself in his cell. The governor attempted to reason with him but to no avail. Eventually the prison warders were forced to batter the door down and poor Rowlands was dragged, kicking and shouting, to the place of execution. As the rope was being secured around his neck he continued to protest his innocence, but his final words were by way of a curse. This was directed at the clock of the nearby church, which he claimed would nor function normally again after his death. The reason for Rowland's behaviour became clear shortly afterwards when another man confessed to the crime.

Dewi Roberts: 'The Land of Old Renown' (1997)

The Column

One of the most notable landmarks in the flat landscape of Ynys Môn is the famous column. This perpetuates the memory of one of the ancestors of the present Marquis of Anglesey who lost his leg while fighting beside the Duke of Wellington. 'By God', the Duke is reported to have said, 'you have lost your leg'. 'By God so I have' was the Marquess' response. The Marquis is represented in Hussar uniform at the top of the column. His lost leg was buried at Waterloo and this inspired the statesman and writer George Canning to write these lines.

Here rests – and let no saucy knave
Presume to sneer or laugh,
To learn that mould'ring in this grave
There lies – a British calf.

For he who writes these lines is sure
That those who read the whole
Will find that laugh was premature;
For here, too, lies the sole.

And here five little ones repose,
Twin born with other five,
Unheeded by their brother toes,
Who all are now alive.

A leg and foot, to speak more plain,
Lie here of one commanding;
Who, though his wits he might retain,
Lost half his understanding;

And when the guns, with thunder fraught,
Poured bullets thick as hail,
Could only in this way be taught
To give the foe leg-bail;

And now in England, just as gay
As in the battle brave,
Goes to the rout, the ball, the play,
With one leg in the grave.

Fortune in vain has showed her spite,
For he will soon be found,
Should England's son engage in fight,
Resolved to stand his ground.

But Fortune's pardon I must beg;
She meant not to disarm;
And when she lopped the hero's leg
She did not seek his h-arm;

And but indulged a harmless whim;
Since he could walk with one,
She saw two legs were lost on him,
Who never meant to run.

George Canning

Plas Newydd, By God

Beneath a polished glass-case
a quirky legend says the fourth
Marquess of Anglesey lost a leg
in the battle of Waterloo.
To a nearby officer he said,
By God, Sir; I have lost my leg.

Saxon *sang-froid* to the fore the former
replied, By God, Sir; so you have.
It's enough, plus Whistler's mural,
to mark this an oddity in our time,
a pile we visit in fast cars,
storming pasts *sans peur et sans reproche.*

By God or by plainer right of Mammon
it may be his wooden leg,
articulated by hidden springs
and overlapping leather straps
or the rooms themselves, filling up
with memorabilia of old battles –

Both field and boudoir – but likelier
is the view from the east terrace,
Snowdon and her companions
shouldering whitely into the first
warm afternoon this late spring.

Clean-lined in snow their silent
being rises where no man may live,
only raven, kestrel, buzzard
cast their patrolling shadows.
Still that leg insists, stiff-lippery
triumphant, class bushido –

By God, Sir; so you have, noted
the other toff, turning back
to survey the more amiable
spectacle of French retreat,

while the shattered leg absorbed
the senses of its former owner.

Propertied by worms, like this Plas now,
the wooden leg's articulacy remains
while we, Joe Public, shuffle round gardens,
throw numbed glances at the Straits and hills.
Indoors, along glitzy blockwood floors,
before Whistler's mural an eager lady
expounds each point of whimsey.

Later we pass the pool where Rex
lolled in Thirties decadence:
Rex, d'you think Hitler *will* invade?
The needle slurred, waves slopped, shone,
hunger queued in Wales, Liverpool,
Spain fell in Laocöon struggle

On a step Whistler left a painted fag
and spectacles; pity he did not raise
them to his time but we remember
his curious flower cut suddenly
in the first landings at Normandy.
The dead can't always bury the dead,
they imprison us with images.

Look at the view, hollow tree, tall yews
splashed with sunlight's yellow water,
so old their time sniffs at our passing feet,
then bury, for a while, your unease
at sweat, necessity, the sheer graft
which built all this, the suffering.

For underneath, that bobbing thought,
like an unsinkable swimmer,
swirls back: that most may crave
perspectives such as these, to enrich,
nurture, their faltering grasp of earth.

Peter Gruffydd

The Reflections of a Cleric

Hugh Jones, who became an Archdeacon of St Asaph, was born in Holyhead. He kept a revealing diary for the years 1832-33. At that time he lived at Beaumaris, from which he made excursions to the wider world beyond. Although he expresses intense Christian fervour in the diary, he also reveals himself as materialistic. The 'exhibition' mentioned below was a grant or scholarship available for aspiring clerics. These extracts appears in print for the first time.

June 22nd 1832: I packed up in order to go by the 'Llewelyn' to Beaumaris. Am terrified by the incidence of the weather, but at length determine upon going. Had a very pleasant sail, though I was rather sick at one point. Reached home about 6-0 in the evening. Clean myself, take tea, and go to hear Mr Robert Newton, who preached at 7-0 for the benefit of the chapel.

September 27th 1832: The trustees of the school met today at whose decision regarding the exhibition I have been exceedingly disappointed as I considered myself more in need than either of those who received them. In consequence of the injustice of the decision my mother has written to the Bishop of Bangor to explain matters to him, which when his Lordship read he expressed great regret that he had not known sooner, but, as it was it could not be undone.

October 3rd 1832: Was this morning surprised and overjoyed at Mr Davies Owen's calling upon me with a note in his hand which he had just received from the Bishop of Bangor enclosing a cheque for £20 to be given to me in lieu of the exhibition. How wonderful are the ways of Providence! How the Almighty can bring good out of evil! Oh God give me a strong trust in thy mercy, fill my soul with gratitude, and grant thy mercies may lead me to repentance.

January 1st 1833: Behold the mercy of God has spared me to see yet another year. Since the last New Years Day how many souls have been hurried into eternity. Alas too many it is to be feared have been sent into the presence of their Maker and their Judge in a state totally unprepared. Shudder my soul at the thought, and let it lead thee to beware that such should be thy case, when the awful hour cometh.

The Rev. Hugh Jones
in his diary

Never Again!

I went over to Amlwch and commenced work. The first sight I had of my new pupils made me regret having ever come there, but it was too late to retract. When the school door was opened in the morning, in rushed a crowd of boys such as I never saw except in a gutter: half of them had no shoes or stockings, most of them had evidently not been washed for some days past, and all were unruly as wild colts. There being no pupil teacher or assistant, I picked out three or four of the most likely looking boys to assist me in bringing some kind of order out of this chaos. After two or three failures, I succeeded at last in getting myself heard, but it was useless to give out any orders in English – that language was utterly unknown to all except two or three English-born boys who had drifted somehow into that out-of-the-way corner. The task before me seemed well-nigh hopeless, but I set to it doggedly; drilling, organizing, classifying. How the late master managed was then a mystery to me. I afterwards found out that he was an easy going man, case-hardened as to noise and confusion, who spent more hours at the 'Ship' than at the school, and left the teaching to take care of itself.

There was a great deal to fight against at Amlwch, enough to frighten a timid man at once, and to cool the zeal of the most determined reformer. Big boys, thoroughly ignorant, brutal in their manners, and disgusting in their habits: parents as ignorant and as brutal, who looked upon the schoolmaster as their natural enemy and resented his attempts at correcting their children's evil habits: no encouragement from outside, not one of the better classes ever entering the school, or taking the slightest interest in it: the clergyman despondent: the laity indifferent or hostile: take it for all in all, I should not like to see its like again.

Robert Roberts: 'The Wandering Scholar' (1923)

William Evans, Llangefni

Often I saw him
Sweeping the empty streets,
Pushing his rusty barrow
Down the gutter.
We lured him with tea
Out of the harsh east wind
Like a squirrel
Persuaded by nuts.

He was nothing remarkable, though,
A little grey man
(His heart the conventional gold)
His thoughts as wholesome as bread –
But without the yeast.

Yet at night, when the beer was flowing,
He knew his glory:
Verse ran from his eager lips
Faster than fire,
Till they gave him a bardic name
And crowned his wonder.
Brwshfab, Son of a Brush –
He knew that they mocked him
But knew that they had no malice:
He bore his title
Proud as a pencerdd down the dusty street.
I doubt if his tombstone bears it –
Or tells his virtue:
Let this, then, honour his music
Who was our friend.

Sally Roberts Jones

Beaumaris Grammar School

Wrapped up in ancient history alongside the castle walls in an old town uniquely situated on the Menai Straits, Beaumaris Grammar School had a special attraction for all its pupils which never left them. The old School was redolent with traditions of bygone days harking back to its founder. David Hughes; many personalities among staff and pupils and the records of sports achievements – football and cricket – in matches with teams from Friars School's, Bangor, Bethesda, Llangefni and Holyhead. Days when we travelled by horse-drawn bus for 'away' matches, at the beginning of this century now so long ago.

My father – Evan Madoc-Jones – took over as headmaster at B.G.S. in 1895 with his wife, Katie. And I first saw the light in their schoolhouse bedroom on May 1st, 1896. Elwyn and Enid, my brother and sister completed the family. And we had the joy of that dear old house and the school premises – with their quaint holes and corners – for playing in. We grew up among the boarders who came from a wide area in North Wales

– as well as from Liverpool. Boarders were housed in upper and lower dormitories – up to 10 or 12 in each. And meals were in the Dining Hall on the ground floor below the 'lower dorm'. Here, too, teas were provided for visiting teams after the games – and especial celebrations on occasions when we had beaten the Friars eleven, in particular – always our great rivals. Our football team's prowess in those early days was remarkable, so we thought, because it was drawn from about 30 pupils.

Father was a great disciplinarian – feared but respected – and had been brought up in the strict Welsh Non-conformist tradition. His parents' roots were deep down in Anglesey and Caernarvonshire, and mother's in Menai Bridge. It is of interest that he was the first Nonconformist to have been appointed to the headship of the school. Previously all headmasters had been of the Anglican faith in conformity with the founder's wishes. On Sundays the boarders used to walk to church and chapel tidy and spruce with our Eton collars and suits to match. After dinner we used to sing hymns in the 'nursery' as it was known – overlooking the garden and the 'pitch' as the school playing field was known – with Baron Hill in the distance; and the Winllan's cluster of trees 'strictly private' in which we roamed when the coast was clear, looking for birds' eggs in season. To get to the pitch one went through the lodge gates where then in the lodge lived an aged caretaker with a wooden leg – well known in his day. He also took payments from visitors going into the castle, if memory serves me aright.

Those days which I am now recalling were simple and down to earth. Pupils would walk to school and back in all weathers from Penmon, Llangoed, Llandegfan, Llanddona and Llan-faes. Some had bicycles. And eventually a bus would carry children from Menai Bridge picking up others en route.

They were times when paperchases were popular events. And on Friday evenings during winter term dances used to be held – organised by my mother – in the school's assembly room and to these the boarders and boys and girls from the town would come, to dance waltzes, lancers and polkas. They were the days when there were two half-holidays – on Wednesdays and Saturdays. Later, of course, Saturday was the weekly holiday. Days when, during the summer term, the old school bell of happy memory would ring out at 7 a.m. for morning school in charge of a member of the teaching staff. Here questions would be asked of the teacher and homework would be done.

I can also recall an event which caused trouble. A notice in the Beaumaris news in the *North Wales Chronicle* reporting a concert in the Town Hall – which had never happened – stating that various members of the school staff had taken part, duets, etc., with some of the then notable 'bad lads' and lasses, characters with local nicknames. The teachers named were furious. Then followed letters to various people signed by some teachers – who had, in fact, not written them. One, following the opening of the Catholic Church, was sent to the Catholic priest requesting that 'for the benefit of her soul' he should call on her. Father called the pupils to the Assembly Hall and demanded that the guilty party should stand-up – or else no half-holiday in the coming week. Nobody stood up. And there was no half-holiday. I can remember one of the masters during a boarders homework session in the boarders' study one night, going carefully through a pile of pupils' class-books and studying letters – one sent to the *Chronicle* and others to members of the staff – in an effort to track down the offender(s). But – without success. Many years afterwards one of the old B.G.S. pupils – when father had retired – called on him. They discussed old times and he told father that he, with three other contemporaries, had been responsible for the several contentious correspondences. And father laughed heartily – thoroughly enjoying the occasion.

Geraint Madoc Jones in the Anglesey
Antiquarian Society Transactions (1971)

A Holyhead Childhood

At the end of the war, when I was nearly six, we moved to Holyhead, where my father had got a job on the Irish ferries. I remember the day we arrived: a dark wet day in December. Is there any town worse than Holyhead on a day like that? The taxi took us along the bare streets to our lodgings, and I stared gloomily through the cab windows. But the next day came and it was a pearl of a morning! Everywhere glistened and the sea was blue as could be. You must know the old penillion:

Ar noswaith ddrycinog mi euthum i rodio
Ar lannau y Fenai gan ddistaw fyfyrio;
Y gwynt oedd yn uchel, a gwyllt oedd y wendon,
A'r môr oedd yn lluchio dros waliau Caernarfon.

Ond trannoeth y bore mi euthum i rodio
Hyd lannau y Fenai, tawelwch oedd yno;
Y gwynt oedd yn ddistaw, a'r môr oedd yn dirion,
A'r haul oedd yn twynnu ar waliau Caernarfon.

There you have a fair description of the sort of weather Anglesey has. Indeed if someone asks you what sort of weather to expect there, tell him: Oh, it'll get better towards the afternoon. The weather was king in Holyhead. It ruled almost all my activities. I was a sickly child in my early teens. My mother believed that enough fresh air would make a new man of me. So for a year I didn't go to school; I stayed in the open air. I wandered through the fields; I played on the river banks; I fished for blennies among the rocks. These were *some* blennies too! I loved the eager way they grabbed at the bait. All that was needed was to put a piece of a limpet on a bent pin, lower it into a small pool, and watch the blenny charge at it from its hiding-place, to be caught by me and put in a jam-jar. I could have fished for hours, but an eye had to be kept on the tide. I was caught more than once, and had to jump through the water to the shore; and then got a good talking to from my mother.

When the time came for me to start school, I met some new friends: a family who lived at the other end of the Island. The mother was a widow, with three children, a girl and two boys. The girl was three years older than me, but the boys were about my age. They lived in Penrhos Fedw, and soon that name came to seem like magic to me. The house stood alone in the fields with the open sea about half a mile away. The boys had places in the gorse where they could hide, completely out of sight – long tunnels leading through the undergrowth to some central chamber, and there we would sit like red Indians to make our plans. My mother and father used to visit their mother quite often, and while they chatted or played cards in the winter, we children would be playing in and out of the house. It was a marvellous experience to sneak out into the darkness sometimes and stand under the stars with the wind from the sea sighing about the silent house. And then we used to walk the two miles or so home through the night, with the gorse creaking on either side of the road, and the occasional shooting-star speeding quietly across the heavens and disappearing like Williams Parry's fox. Safely in bed, I would go to sleep to the sound of the singing of a group of locals who used to gather sometimes on the corner of the street behind our house.

In the summer I would go over to my friends even more often. There was a good spot for bathing nearby, an inlet called Porth Gof Du, and it was there we liked to go. They were like porpoises in the water and I quickly learnt to swim. It was a perfect place, and completely private. Very rarely would there be anyone else there. When the tide came in there would be about six foot of water in the sandy trough which formed the inlet. The water was crystal-clear, and the fish-spawn and sand-eels stood out blue in its depths. The inlet faced east, and on many a morning

I saw the sea shining like silver or gold in the sun. On mornings like these, our hearts were light and full of fun, and we would sing at the top of our voices along the path through the heather to the inlet. Certainly there was some magic in the sea there, and the body cried out to be baptised in it. Other times, in the afternoon when the inlet was in the shade, after a quick swim we would get dressed and go to explore the cliffs. I didn't have such a good head for heights as my friends and I would often have to turn back, only to be called a coward. But I eventually learnt how to look over the edge of the cliff without being frightened too much, and discovered that there was a fairly easy way down after all. It was a delight to climb down to some small remote beach, with the cliffs like a wall around us, and to feel that no-one had ever stood there before. And the seagulls would add to that feeling, circling overhead making a deafening noise. Sometimes, to disprove our belief that we were the first there, we would come across an iron ring. But we would soon decide that pirates had fixed it there! Have you ever heard the sound of the sea in a little rocky cove? There is no sound like it; or like the hollow smack of a wave penetrating the deep recesses of the rock. This was true solitude, and even three lively and mischievous boys would become quieter under its influence. Then a race up to the top of the cliff; sometimes getting stuck because we had taken a wrong turning. The only thing to do then was to go back and start again, although the top of the cliff was only a few yards away. The perfect end to a day like that in the summer, was to walk home through a twilight full of the smell of grass and honeysuckle and the song of the nightjar in the bracken. My skin would be stinging from the sun and salt sea; but a glass of water before going to bed tasted marvellous, and the white sheets were smooth and refreshing.

R.S. Thomas: 'Selected Prose' Edited by Sandra Anstey (1983)

Fairyland

Llanrhuddlad and Llanfair-yng-Nghornwy were a fairyland to a small boy, and everywhere I felt the presence of my dead forebears. *Taid* seemed to be everywhere and the faces of everyone, Church and Nonconformist alike, lit up at the mention of his name. Ten years, twenty years after his death, he was still the old Chancellor, and his memory was worshipped in the parish. Old men and old women would tell endless stories of *Taid* and *Nain*.

We used to visit farms for *crempog* teas and I used to eye the huge pot of melted butter, in which lurked the small round pancakes, with apprehension. I knew I could never eat enough to satisfy the farmer's wife, and always when I had consumed about six I could take no more. Unfortunately one's manhood was judged by one's capacity to down a vast number of *crempogau* and I always failed abysmally in the eyes of the parish.

'Well, well, you are no good,' complained one old body. 'Your father could do twelve, Master Johnny could do twenty and your grandfather twenty-four.'

I was humiliated and hardly a member of the rector's family anymore.

'*Dduw*, Master John, only six? Well, well, you're hopeless.'

There would be laughter and cheerful goodbyes, but I crept away, a six-*crempog* boy.

It was a glorious place for a summer holiday. Gentle farms, and steep cliffs covered with gorse and heather; and in the spring the grassy slopes above the sea were coated with sea pinks and a pale-blue smoke of delicate scilla. Narrow lanes dived between high grass-topped banks that hid the gentle, munching Welsh blacks. The noise as they invisibly tore the sweet grass conjured up images of strange beasts. Sometimes they were elephants or buffaloes, bison or prehistoric animals.

The farm we liked best was Swtan. Everything was thatched there, the outbuildings, the pigsties and the squat little farmhouse with its mighty tower-like chimney at one end. 'Swtan' is a strange name, and long ago it used to be called 'Swittan', which reinforces the legend that Suetonius Paulinus landed there, for the 'w' is pronounced more forcibly in Welsh than it is in English.

When we stayed at Llanrhuddlad, old Hugh Jones lived there, as he had when my father was a boy. He was in his eighties when I knew him, a tall dignified figure with an iron-grey beard that emerged from beneath a black trilby hat. He farmed the few acres and fished in the bay below.

I remember one evening he took Dick and me out into the bay in his boat, and there, gazing towards the shore, he gave what amounted to a running commentary on the landing of Suetonius from his galleys. Under the spell of Hugh Jones' vivid and dramatic description I could see it all happening. Bearded, bronze-clad figures leaped from their galleys, centurions, infantrymen and finally the mighty Suetonius himself. There was a savage battle as my ancestors hurled spears and stones from the cliff-tops until, inevitably, a terrible massacre took place on the slopes of the Garn. My excitement was dampened by the feeling that Hugh Jones seemed to favour the Romans.

Swtan has long been deserted, and its ruins lie like the decomposing body of a rabbit, the thatch and rafters like a jumble of hair and bones.

Down at Porth Swtan there was sand and many-coloured cliffs, and deep rock pools with glorious starfish and sea anemones, while out at sea the grey shapes of the liners slipped by towards the Skerries, from where they would turn eastwards to Liverpool. Their great engines throbbed, and we waited for the wash to break on the sandy shore. There were days when a heavy sea-mist drenched and clung to the land, blotting out the comforting bulk of Holyhead mountain across the bay. The ships wailed and crept anxiously by while an air of mystery cloaked the land.

Kyffin Williams: 'Across the Straits' (1973)

Pentrepella – Kyffin Williams

'nid yw'r graig yn siarad Saesneg'
'the rocks don't understand English' – Bethesda saying

Like mud from the beudy
it was not to be brought indoors,
the language farmers used
to talk about bulls and the birth of calves.
Even your father,
who only came alive in Welsh,
had to scrape it off at the doorstep.

Taidi's house – one patched eye,
the other stuck to his telescope –
was kind to the old words that dawdled
among thrift, sea campion,
crempot teas on the farms, and the Liverpool liners
washing the Skerries.

But grandfather's – who relished his diary:
'No sermon today, owing to my throat.
The year ends with gloomy prospect,
owing to Transvaal war' –
could not stomach their half-dressed carollings and chirpings.

School in Trearddur, where the wind slipped its tracts
under the doors of holiday cottages.
Days on the hills with Bonzo,
or loafing on Moel y Gest in the sun.
Then the lost years of elocution
at Shrewsbury, four mile runs
and beatings over hot water pipes.
After a botched tonsillectomy
you gave up trying
and drifted as far from words
as your eyes could carry.

Your brother started his career.
They found you articles with Yale and Hardcastle
off the High Street, Pwllheli.
Land agents of the old school –
mornings tootling round the estates,
then a meet with the Border Counties
or a rough shoot at Nanhoron.
One night in the Anglesey Arms –
You'd been out after duck on the Afon Wen –
a glass of port, Sospan Fach, the Old Grey Mare –
you woke under the snow
on your bedroom floor,
blood in your mouth, your tongue
a bolster stuffed with pain.

The doctor prescribed
Belladonna, luminal, Irish Moss;
gave instructions not to use your brain
to excess. You joined the Royal Welsh Fusiliers
as a Second Lieutenant.
The War took you from Pwllheli to Porthmadog,
across the water to Lurgan
and back, your troops labelled
'Passenger to Pwllheli. I speak no English.'
Six months at Maentwrog
pretending what to do
if the Germans came.
But no dodging the Grand Mal.
'You can't play sir, you're not well,'

as they carried you foaming
from the rugby field.
The medical board found you abnormal
and discharged you to the Slade.

A half world of the Home Guard
and figure drawing.
Three days teaching a week.
You found it comfy, having no talent
and no-one to push you.
On dull evenings
drawn by the light behind a roof ridge,
the sheen of wet slate,
you painted your way to Wales.
Even Miss Jopling's half-blind cooking –
bread, butter and marmalade cat hairs,
your morning kipper grilled
in the News of the World –
could not stop you following hounds
down tongues of water
after make-believe otters.

You watched the cliffs break against the sea
at Capel Tywyn,
slept where the Ynysfor taps
gushed midnight Guinness.
At Bisham Gardens, N6, you learned
to talk to the rocks
in their own language.

Bryan Aspden

Lord Cledwyn

Lord Cledwyn has since childhood been steeped in the social, religious
and political history of Anglesey. The family hearth also provided him
with a rich inheritance of radical Labourite values and an appreciation of
the wealth of Welsh-language culture derived from the quarrying
districts of Dinorwig and Llanrug in Caernarfonshire, where his mother
and father were born and brought up. The independence of spirit,
associated with the slate-quarrying communities, has also been a

prevalent feature of his personality, as was evident, too, in his father's life and values. He also inherited from his father a contrasting characteristic, the pastoral skill of seeking compromise and reconciliation. From his father, a slate quarryman in his early days, he also, undoubtedly, inherited his verbal dexterity and love of anecdote, perhaps derived from the customary banter of the quarrymen's cabin.

However, it was his upbringing in Anglesey which was the major influence on Lord Cledwyn. As a young boy, he was acquainted with two of his predecessors as M.P. for Anglesey – Sir R.J. Thomas and Megan Lloyd George, and he also steeped himself in the history of their predecessors, among them Sir Ellis Jones Griffith and Thomas 'Palesteina' Lewis. His father was a friend of such prominent figures in the island's religious circles as Dr John Williams, Brynsiencyn, and other mainstays of the Anglesey of old. 'Gwŷr Mawr Môn' – the 'Great Men of Anglesey' – were often the topic of discussion at his childhood home at 'Y Frondeg', Holyhead.

Emyr Price: 'Lord Cledwyn of Penrhos' (1990) Translated by Chris Jones

---

This poem relies on a well-known convention of Welsh poetry, the llatai or love-messenger, whereby the poet sends an animal or bird with a message to his love. It appears here for the first time.

SENDING A HARRIER TO
LLANEILIAN

I.M. Bedwyr Lewis Jones,
Professor of Welsh at Bangor

Cantref of Cemaes

1

Low over the rough pasture, dark harrier,
As if you'd lost a key
You search dank ground.

Flap slowly upwind, tread air . . .
You grip your wings
Like a divining rod.

Their shallow V dips
As you peer
Into reed and rush.

Momentarily you hover, your white skirts
Swirling, turn
To focus on a vole.

Delicate, murderous hands
Prepare to drop . . .
Not this time, though!

A twitch of impatience – and the huge
Fingering wings
Shrug it off,

Flap to regain
Inertia . . . Your problems
Are those of scholarship,

The aeronautics of slowness
In a featureless
Terrain –

For a yard at a time, to read
With your magnifying eye
Black-letter of earth.

2

Hen harrier, as I watch you
The memory
Of Bedwyr
Flicks through the pages.

I've lost a key
From my ring –
A key to openhanded
Welshness,

A key to the hospitality
Of Tywyn and Nannau.
I've lost a scholar,
Vade mecum of learning.

A key to priest-lofts,
To glory-holes,
Civilization
In brown almanacs.

I've lost a protector.
A key to the wardship
Of Wales, a hearth
Open as day.

A key to compassion,
To justice.
A key to the validity
Of Bangor in the world.

3

Hawk, if you'd find that key
Where it hides
In the crevices
Of grass . . .

Imagine you, wandering
In search of it,
Migrating
To the good lands,

Beating west-nor'-west
Across the westerlies,
Climbing to trip thermals
On the Carneddi,

Till all the variety
Of Gwynedd
Lies twisted and knuckled
At the edge of your eyes.

There's the long scabbard
Of Menai,
Decorated
With dinghies.

You're a dragon now,
Rummaging Wales
For a home, a courage,
A hospitality . . .

A tower with a pyramid spire –

Llaneilian
Like a galleon embattled
Towing a coracle –

The cell of its saint.

4

Musics of the tongue,
Of plucked strings,
Of chiselled wood.

Tracery of words, phonemes, syllables.
Tracery of pitch, tone-lengths, rhythm.
Tracery of uprights, curves, vineleaves . . .

The carved rood-loft
Like all traditional things
Waits to be used.

It dominates the nave
Not for itself, but to service
A cross long ago gone –

To illuminate,
To emblaze with candles
The hanging God.

A loft for musicians –
Look, two are carved
Under the beams,

With flute (is it?) and bagpipe,
The wide chanter
Wrapped by his hands.

And though their lips breathe
And they finger the notes,
Their eyes stare out:

Two stolid angels
As they play, look through us
To an ecstasy

That would burn,
Would char our eyes
In the brightness of their dark.

5

Scholar, this is the place.
Fly, elbow your wings
Round the green enclosure.

The key's here
Surely, in this mediaeval yard
Where the graves

Of children and wives, poets and farmers,
– God's acre –
Go back a millenium

To the saint himself,
Eilian
And the ruined spring –

Surely you'll find it . . .
See there, by the wall
Is Bedwyr's rest.

No, nothing's here.
Neither key nor opening –
Nothing!

– Only inside the church, a grotesque
Jabbering death,
A man of bone

Painted on the rood-loft,
For the first time
Claims our acquaintance –

Memento mori
With a wink of an empty socket
And a whistle of dry wind.

Tony Conran

Language Protest, Llangefni

It isn't even dramatic
Two shivering boys
Stood on a broad, flat roof,
The police themselves
Don't bother to force the issue.

They are free to come
Or to go:
We burn no martyrs
(For all of it's done in our name)
But learnt from Casement
How to discredit heroes –

The quiet whisper
'Iwan's a petty thief'.
The glib assumption
Their cause is a mere insanity, their love
A strait-jacket passion
For out-dated gods.

Those two young boys,
Misguided perhaps, won't find
Anything more than a moment slipped between
Ulster and Africa:
Won't rot in an English gaol
For their love's persistence –
May find in an English lodging
Their only home.

Plaster the hills with hiraeth,
The roads with sign-posts
Fully approved, bilingual –
But also, first,
Make sure that those signs don't point
Forever east.

Sally Roberts Jones

This short story is set during a period in the nineteen eighties when the ownership of second homes in Wales was a very contentious issue, resulting in arson attacks on some of these dwellings by nationalist extremists.

The Sea Book
a short story by Glenda Beagan

It was like a young shark. Lithe, streamlined, with a fierce face.

'What is it?' Gavin asked.

'I dunno,' said Heather.

'It'll die if it stays there.'

'No it won't, stupid. When the tide comes in it'll swim off, won't it?'

'But it's going to get worn out. It's going to hurt itself. Look.'

And she looked. Despite herself. Wrinkling up her face as the creature lashed and fought against the rock. The air was full of the sharp crack of its tail and arching back. She wanted to close her eyes. Get away from here. The shallow water trapping it in the pool, the crack between the layered slabs, seemed to sting, to burn with its fury.

'We'll have to save it.'

'How?'

She heard the sound of her voice become hard, contemptuous. She heard the sneer in it. Why did she have to put up with him all the time? Drag him around everywhere? This place was boring now. She didn't see why she had to come here at all. Why wouldn't they let her go and stay with Claire and Miriam in Guildford?

'I'm going to try and save it.'

'It'll bite you. You'll fall in or something and they'll blame me. Why can't you leave things alone?'

Gavin wasn't listening. He was crouched down on the rocks staring hard at the fish thing as it writhed.

'I just wish we could tell it to wait. To be quiet and wait for the tide.'

'That's what I said. But it's stupid isn't it? It's like you. It hasn't got a brain.'

Again he ignored her. It was difficult to get a foothold near enough, among all the weed. Bladderwrack with its blobs for popping. Slithery thongweed. Where could he grip? By the tail? It was big though, wasn't it? And slippery. And it wasn't in the best of tempers.

He'd thought it out. You could tell. Heather wanted to walk away. Leave him. But she couldn't. There he was, like a Red Indian or something, crouched there. Oblivious of her. Oblivious of everything. And she knew, deep down inside, that Gavin was simply better than she was. He was different, yes, but it was more than that. More than their mother would allow. She always said they were chalk and cheese and made a joke about it. But it wasn't funny. At all.

Around them the sea, the sky, the sounds of the estuary. Oystercatchers making their tinny cry. Was it a sad cry? Was it happy? She couldn't decide. Anymore than she could decide whether the lighthouse on its thin, and from here almost invisible, island was something she loved or hated. She turned back to him. She wanted to say something spiteful. But she couldn't. In a horrible way, she knew Gavin was good. Simply good. And knowing that made her feel small and mean inside.

'I've got him.'

Gavin's shout, Gavins' running, was everywhere. The whole place, the rocks, the clouds, the air, was full of Gavin. And the fish thing, that was Gavin too, as he went hurtling off over the glittering wet stones of the promontory, with it wriggling, fighting in his grip. Almost slipping, almost flat on his face, but catching himself as he started to fall, swivelling back upright, then on again, until, just at the point where the stones filtered out, and the deep channel of the river, narrow and deep, a dark green, almost black, reached the sea, he stopped, raising both hands with the great slippery fish thing between them, and flung. And as the fish hit the water there was a sound like a door slamming, or a gun going off. A sideways, steady fling, with hardly a splash, so the fish joined the current at just the right angle, in just the right place.

'You should've seen it,' he said, catching up with her, breathless, as she picked her way back. 'It was brilliant. Just like it was flying.' And it wasn't as if he was showing off or anything. He wasn't like that. He just wanted to share it with her. 'Great,' she said, struggling. And then he was off again, running back to the house, past the upturned boats pulled high up on the sandy bit.

* * *

It was Heather answered the phone. It didn't matter who answered it. It shouldn't have mattered. But it did. It was Mrs Evans, and she asked to speak to Dr Penry, so Heather knew something was wrong. Mrs Evans had only phoned once before and that was after the gales, when the big ash tree had fallen and smashed the greenhouse. There weren't many tall trees on Anglesey, she'd said, as if in some way having a tall tree was wrong. This was worse, though. Heather just knew. You could tell by her voice.

'He's not in at the moment,' Heather said. 'Can I give him a message?'

'Is your mother there, dear?'

'Yes. I'll get her.'

Afterwards they sat in stunned silence. Heather couldn't stand it. Especially the look on Gavin's face.

'It's all my fault,' she said at last, gulping it out, her fingers over her mouth like a claw.

'What on earth makes you think that? Darling, I know you're upset, but really . . . '

'It is my fault. It's because of me. I didn't want to go last time, did I? I wanted to stay with Claire and Miriam.'

'But that hasn't got anything to do with it. You surely don't think it has . . .'

Then Gavin started to charge round the room. 'I'll kill them,' he said. 'I'll strangle them with my bare hands. I will. I'll get them. I'll find out where they live and I'll burn their houses down.'

'Now that's enough, the pair of you. Really. This doesn't help. We don't know the extent of the damage yet. It may not be that bad. And you can be sure your father's got the place insured properly.'

Gavin stared open-mouthed at his mother. 'That's not the point. Whether it's insured or not. You just don't understand, do you? You make me sick. If they had to burn somewhere I wish they'd burnt this place. I hate it. Llwyn Onn was my great grandfather's house.'

'I do know that Gavin. I don't think you need to tell me the family history.'

'But you're not a Penry, are you?'

'No, but I am your mother and I won't be spoken to like that.'

'Stop it. For God's sake stop it,' said Heather. 'This is terrible. I wish Daddy was here.'

'So do I. Now just sit down, Gavin. No, better than that, go and make us all a cup of tea. And you can put a drop of whisky in it. For all of us. Yes, for medicinal purposes. And if you think you're old enough to take up the cudgels over matters of family honour, you're old enough to start behaving with a modicum of realism and common sense. And that's a Mainstone speaking. And you can stop looking at me like that.'

Gavin glowered and stormed off to the kitchen. Heather just sat there. Squirming. Listening to the tea things being thumped and banged around. This wasn't how Gavin behaved. She was supposed to be the one with the temper. Everything had been turned upside down.

What did it look like? The house? She saw what Mr Evans must have seen when he got up to see why the dog was barking. She saw the roof of Llwyn Onn ablaze, and then her eyes seemed to sink down through the flames and the smoke, right down to the lean-to at the back. Gavin's den, where he kept all his things. Hers too, since she'd told him she'd grown out of all those old jigsaws and board games. They'd kept them amused when it rained, yes, but he could have them now. It was babyish to want them at all, to still be interested.

And then he saw The Sea Book. Little pink flames like cats' tongues were licking the covers, mended with sticky tape, the spine split right through and glued and glued again. It had belonged to their father, and his before that. Gavin loved it. He'd only been small when he'd discovered it, calling it The Hairloom, pronouncing the 'H' very grandly and deliberately, making them laugh.

She thought of that last day on the shore, the day he'd saved the fish. Then she saw him sat in the den's one huge chair, the book on his knee. He was just like a wizard poring over his spells. 'Here it is,' he said, 'Look, I've got it. It's a lesser spotted dogfish. This is it, exactly. Like a small shark. That's what it says.' And he'd looked up at her, all eagerness. And she'd frozen him out. Like she always did. And it wasn't as if she wanted to do it. She didn't. It made her feel hellish. But she did it just the same.

Why did she feel like this? About Gavin. About Llwyn Onn. The things, the people who meant the most to her. Why did she treat them so badly? It was like a judgement, this burning. Somehow it would have helped to think there really was a God up there, and that this was a punishment. Gavin came into the room carrying the tray. He put it down on the coffee table. Very quietly. Around his mouth the skin was tight

154

and pale. Heather looked at her mother. Couldn't she see it? Didn't she care?

'Get the whisky please, Gavin,' she said.

It was just like watching a play. Gavin brought the decanter from the bureau. Slowly, theatrically, he poured a little whisky into each steaming cup. It was ridiculous. Heather wanted to laugh. Or cry. Or scream. Do something. Didn't dare. And it wasn't just the burning of the house. All this. Whatever it was that was happening.

* * *

'Are you sure you want to go over now? It's not going to be too upsetting for you, is it? I wouldn't want that, not after telling your father I'd look after you here. And Elfed says it's not a pretty sight.'

'Gavin's gone Mrs Evans. I don't know why I should have to stay. They didn't want me to come at all but I said it would be worse not seeing.'

'Well there is that. Yes. Imagining things is worse sometimes. But I think it's a pity your mother isn't here with you, myself.'

'She can't be here. She's got a preview at the gallery.'

'Well, maybe, but I still say she should have come. I told her on the phone it can't be anyone local. She mustn't think that, I said. Local people know quite well who your father is. And there's many remember how your grandfather, when he started off, worked with old Dr Lloyd-Jones in Amlwch. Elfed's got a cousin in an old people's home in Llangefni swears it was your great-grandfather loaned them money in the twenties. When times were very bad. Speaks very highly of him. And I've never heard a word said against any of you. Not one. So I told Mrs Penry, I said, you mustn't think badly of us. No one local wanted this to happen.'

'No,' said Heather. 'Anyway, I want to see for myself.'

She left Mrs Evans hovering in the door and walked the long way round. Heavy rain overnight had left deep puddles in the lane. Yellow leaves were floating. And as she turned by the hedge the gable end of Llwyn Onn reared up, looking strangely normal. From this angle it was all a bad joke. Nothing seemed to have happened. Then the front of the house.

Roof fallen in. Charred rafters. The bones of a dinosaur. Black round the windows, smudged against whitewash. Weird. The face of the toy panda on guard in their den. Sat in the big chair. But she'd felt it all when the phone call came. Seen it too. The cats' tongue flames. This was cold somehow. Cold and unreal.

Voices inside. Mr Evans. Her father. No sign of Gavin, but she knew where he'd be.

155

Past the moored boats. Everything shining. The peeling paint, the sand with glints in it. Crushed shells. Silence. Almost. Just the swishing sound of waves far away. A mist offshore. Hiding the island, the lighthouse. Then the sharp sound of feet on the rocks. Gavin running, carrying something.

'Wait,' she shouted.

But he couldn't hear. Wouldn't have stopped anyway. Looking so small against the bowl of the sky. I'm sorry, she told herself. Sorry for everything, Gavin. I don't mean the things I say. Mostly.

He was standing where he'd stood on the day of the dogfish. In just the same place. And she knew what he was doing. And why. Though there weren't any words to explain.

He paused for a moment, then threw it. What was left of it. Calm. Strong. The right thing to do. And she watched, strangely comforted, walking slowly towards him over the weed.

from 'The Medlar Tree' (1992)

Change

When I came back
There was frost on the road
But I held the first snowdrop,
A star on my brow.
In my parents' window
The light was out.
My friends' laughter
Teased behind hedges –
I chased
And found the shadowed snow.

'This is my home,' I cried –
It echoed on the night.
'This is my island home.'

I scanned the landscape like a foreign language
And found a noun I knew, a farm upon a hill,
Embedded in an alien syntax

Marianne Jones

The Shock

At Anglesey, one childhood holiday,
I feared to enter the mouth of a rose
opening its red cavern on the wallpaper
of a farm guest-house. Shy in the extreme,
I also feared to scream, nightmaring silently.
That week, off Bull Bay, I saw
the sleek seals' heads
bobbing like dark corks;
and I was told, at Red Wharf Sands,
of the murdered woman buried there –
her head was missing, perhaps anywhere
under the beach. I remembered
when I reached for my spade,
made no sand-castles, trod warily:
even the seashells were suspect
like the sand, no longer bland.
On the headland, every branch
held a snail under the leaves
and my Auntie's matchbox contained
an earwig. Back for the farmhouse meal
I refused to eat rabbit, rejected the pink pie.

Returning to the sooty sunlight of the city,
the evening sandstone warm and welcoming
in my Grandmother's backyard, I saw her dear bulk
bending over a bucket and, on coming closer,
the sleek wet bodies of kittens
bobbing like dark corks,
here and there a face floating,
the slit eyes, ears all innards,
mouths silently mewing –
the shock, in sunlight, seeing
my Grandmother drowning kittens.

Gladys Mary Coles

Bonfire Night

Bonfire night and I'm in with the dogs.
Alice hides in the toilet. Oscar doesn't:
He charges the length of the house, jitterbugs

At the window, raises roaring comment
With his tail sprung and his body bristling.
Across Llyn Maelog, fires blaze like beacons

Or bombed out holiday homes; rockets go whistling
Up into sky-night, to burst bellies of light, aliens
To scoff at the stars for one climaxing moment.

A machine gun rattles, there are crackles, pops, and snaps
Like over-amplified Rice Crispies. This is a war zone, testament
To all the noise man can make, bangers, fizgigs: lock up your pets.

I am unimpressed by this flex of muscle, this magnificent feat,
This shot-gun display. My mother says they went to sleep
Under tables when the air-raid sirens wailed. Erased whole streets.

Fiona Owen

Interlude at Traeth Bychan

It was the summer of *The Magus*.

He did what men do when they are young
beside the sea – lazed or swam,
anointed himself with oil,
watched children digging, quarrelling,
building castles with tacky sand
which they or the sea would soon flatten.
Timeless tides came and went.

He opened the book on a second island
where a labyrinth swallowed him.
There was a magician with a revolver,
there was a girl, slim and elusive.

He floated in another sea,
was tanned by another sun.
He read: *Greece is like a mirror.*

Flank to flank, in a black bikini,
she lay sleeping or half-asleep.
Freckles scattered across her skin.
Her dark hair dropped to her shoulders,
letting the sunlight lacquer it.
In the lenses of her sunglasses,
his eyes looked back at him.

At night they took the cliff path
to the village with the one pub. The beer
disgusted them. They returned beneath
a peach-slice of moon, generous stars.
Catching at their clothing, brambles
had to be unhooked. And the sea? Always
hushing itself, it never seemed to sleep –

unlike the two of them in the caravan
in the quarry out of sight of the bay,
tired by love-making and the inertia of the day.
It was a story without a plot, just
a simple narrative. It directed him to wake
to a sunny island's tumbled rocks,
blue water, a girl with brown hair

and a book with unread pages.

Richard Poole

Editor's note: The reference in the opening line is to John Fowles' novel 'The Magus', which was published in the sixties. It has a Greek setting.

Blind Date
a short story by Jane Edwards
translated by Derec Llwyd Morgan

I've borrowed this frock from Gwen; it's a pink one with a mauve velvet ribbon around the waist. Everybody knows it's a choir frock, but it's prettier than the one I've got, though it's much too big and miles too long. I've been standing for hours in the glass, studying myself, turning and twisting the frock all ways to see if I can make it look better. Gwen has warned me not to pin it in or tack the hem. It's that sort of material that shows everything.

'What if we lapped the waist like this over the ribbon,' said Gwen, 'and pretend that it's a blouse and skirt you've got.' But to no avail. 'Don't worry,' said Gwen, 'I'll lend you my high heels. It won't look so long then.'

'I'm not size fours yet,' I said peevishly.

Then we heard Margaret's voice talking with Mam in the kitchen. 'Comb your hair. I'll go and tell her you won't be two hoots,' said Gwen.

Margaret had on her a brand-new frock not yet out of its creases. A yellow one, with butterflies. 'Pretty. New?' I asked.

'From the club,' she answered, 'a big parcel from Littlewoods arrived on the L.M.S. yesterday.'

'Lucky you,' I said, turning to look at Mam.

She was feeding the baby, and struggling to tuck one breast under her clothes before getting the other out. Her teats were long and red and dripping. I really don't know why she couldn't have gone to the parlour to feed. I'd say *teats* was the ugliest word in the world.

'You've had a bath,' I told Margaret, seeing her nose shining and her blonde hair a cluster of curls on her shoulders. She lives in a council house. About a year ago all the council houses got a bathroom with hot water heated from the fire, and a toilet with a chain outside. We get our bath in the wash-house every other Saturday when Mam puts a fire under the boiler. It's ever so warm there. You can't see farther than the tip of your nose for steam. Dad still holds that there's nothing like a bath in front of a roaring great fire. But Mam says this is more private, and that it's important for us to keep with the times. 'That costs money,' says Dad. He's an old spendthrift. He'd be astounded to know that the bath costs three pounds ten. Mam pays half a crown weekly, by postal order.

'Where did you get that pink lipstick?' I asked Margaret.

'Borrowed some from Helen next door,' she said. 'I'm going to buy some next time I go to Woolworth. Outdoor Girl: only costs tenpence.' I'd be ever so glad if Mam believed in buying a new one instead of that red

160

thing that tastes old like Adam.

'Are you ready now?' Margaret asked. She was looking at her watch as if she was on tenterhooks.

'What's the hurry? Nothing calls,' said Mam.

'Doesn't she know then?' said Margaret when we were out of the entry.

'Gracious me no, or none of my feet would be out. Does your mother know?'

'She never bothers.'

We walk for a while without saying a word. That's the effect talking about mothers has on you.

Margaret said: 'That pink suits your suntan.'

'It's a bit big though.'

Margaret is a tall well-built girl and I'm a small skinny scrag. And when we walk together everyone turns his head to look at us. But because it's Saturday night there aren't so many about. Neli Harriet as usual is in the telephone kiosk. Looking for lovers, that's what she's doing,' said Margaret, they call it Neli Harriet's bungalow.'

Then Deina Jones Tyddyn toddles out of her house, a stained shawl over her shoulders. She stands stunned-like in our path, thrusts her nose into our faces. 'And where are you two going on a Saturday night like this, all made up as there never were a pair?'

'Date,' Margaret boasted.

'Points at your age! Home scrubbing floors or learning verses, that's your place. Does your mother know?' she asked me.

'She will now,' said Margaret, stepping out of her way.

'Is that a choir frock you're wearing?' she asked, feeling the stuff with her forefinger and thumb.

'Cheek!' I said to Margaret.

'A real busybody.'

It was beginning to get chilly by now. The sun had gone behind a cloud, and a breeze was blowing a leaf or two across the street.

'Where's that pretty green frock with long sleeves you had?' said Margaret.

'The one that made a paper noise? Gone too small.' It was Bill who liked that frock. 'I like your frock,' he said one afternoon as we stood by Nelson's Tower looking at the others throwing stones into the river. 'It makes a noise like tissue paper.' His voice was different as if he were hoarse, or as if it were nearly breaking. 'Mam made it,' I said shyly, and left him. We didn't speak to each other for weeks afterwards. And we're still a bit bashful.

161

'I've got a pen-friend,' said Margaret. She pulled a piece of paper from her pocket. 'Through Radio Luxembourg. Perhaps I'll write to him tomorrow. Terry's his name, Terry Wayne O'Brien. Here's his address.'

'I like your handwriting,' I said.

'From London.'

'So I see. Gee, you've got good handwriting. Much better than mine. Everyone's saying you should have passed scholarship.'

'No one to push me.'

A kick for me, that one.

'Would you like Terry to find you a pen-friend?'

She was saying the name *Terry* as if she'd known him all her life. I honestly didn't like the way she said it.

'I wouldn't dare. Mam would half murder me.'

'Needn't worry, he could put his letter in with Terry's. We wouldn't be any the worse for trying. Perhaps he'd get a student for you.'

A student. Like Mr Harrington, who came to teach us Scripture and biology. Mr Harrington from somewhere far away like Surrey, his hair yellow as gold, his eyes blue and soft. Mr Harrington who was always so kind and tender. Mr Harrington who would duck under the desk every time he heard an aeroplane. Mr Harrington.

Margaret said, 'You're very quiet.'

'I was thinking.'

'Thought so. Perhaps you're nervous.'

'A little.'

'You're shivering.'

'Cold.'

'You should eat more. I get two dinners every day. School dinner and another when Dad gets home.'

That's why she's bonny. I can't stand food. That's why I'm scraggy.

'Perhaps I'd better nip home and fetch my cardigan.'

'There's no time. The boys won't wait for us. Hey, do you like my scent? It's Evening in Paris.' She lifts her hair so that I can sniff behind her ear.

'Mmm . . . nice. Nain had some of that from Auntie Meri as a Christmas box. A small blue bottle with the Eiffel Tower on it. Nain only uses it for chapel. Two spots on her handkerchief.'

'You're not supposed to put scent on clothes.'

'Leusa says the nuns say that only people who don't wash use scent,' I said, to stop her having the last word every time.

'Huh! They need it. Do you know what I hear?'

'What?'

'That they go to bed in their clothes.'

'Never!'

'Do you know what else I heard? They daren't look at themselves in a glass or in a shop-window, or look at their breasts when they change underwear.'

'I don't either,' I said shyly.

'Well, you should. How will you know one isn't bigger than the other? Or that you haven't got three like that woman in the *News of the World*?'

The *News of the World* is terrible. It's got stories to raise the hair on your head, and keep you awake all night. True stories about women turning into men and men turning into women, and every calamity that could hit you.

I've got goose pimples all over me. My inside is shaking like a jelly. My feet are like ice blocks and my scalp is tight and hard. My nose is red. Red and ugly as usual.

I said, 'What about turning back?'

'Turning back? No fear. Afraid or something?'

It's easy for her to talk: she knows this Frank boy. Been with him before. But not one of us has ever seen Henri, though she seems to think he's a farm-hand.

A farm-hand! My dreams don't include farm-hands. My dreams turn round students. Tall handsome students with long scarves around their necks. Students with piles of books under their arms. Merry, noisy students like those I see from the bus at Bangor. Nice respectable students – ministerials like the ones who come for a walk with us to Llyn Rhos Ddu before evening service. Like Mr Harrington.

'How old is this Henri?' I asked as we neared Fern Hill.

'Same age as Frank, I suppose.'

'How old is Frank?'

'Twenty-one.'

'Twenty-one? Heavens above, that's old.'

'You've moaned enough about schoolboys being too young for you. Don't worry. Everything will be all right as long as you don't let Henri put his tongue in your mouth.'

'Put his tongue in my mouth? Ugh!'

'It's a boy's place to try, a girl's place to refuse him.'

'Does Frank try?'

'Every boy tries.'

'What did *you* do?'

'Tell him not to.'

'And he listened?' If anyone tried it on me he'd never see the colour of me again.

'Of course he did. Do you know Olwen? Do you know what Olwen did to a boy from Llangefni way last Saturday night?' She looks into the quick of my eyes and smiles. 'She bit off a piece of his tongue.'

'Bit it off?' I can't swallow because there's a lump like a potato in my throat.

'He had to go to hospital for four stitches.'

I feel quite ill, am cold all over from thinking what I'd do should this boy Henri try such nonsense. Henri's a silly name. An old-fashioned, ugly name. A name to put anybody to shame. How can anyone with a name like that be handsome?

'Why?' I asked coyly, 'why do boys want to put their tongues in your mouth?'

'To make you sleep, of course.'

'Oh!'

'And while you're asleep they lift up your clothes, pull down your knickers, and give you a baby.'

I feel my legs giving under me. I feel my inside caving in. I was always a one for jibbing it.

'I'm not coming,' I said, looking in the roadside for a comfortable place to sit.

'Don't talk rot. Come on,' said Margaret, taking hold of my cold hand with her warm white hand. It was like a picture of a hand in a catalogue.

'I'm shivering,' I said and showed her my arms. 'Look how cold I am. I'd better go home before I catch pneumonia.'

'You won't, stupid. Henri'll warm you up like a piece of toast. Anyway, it's too late for you to turn back now.'

It's never too late. Never ever ever too late. I can run as if the devil himself was after me.

'I can hear a motor bike coming,' said Margaret. 'It's them, I tell you. Here, straighten your frock.'

It's Frank who owns the motor bike. 'Hello, girls,' he says after slapping the pedal with his heel and raising his goggles to have a look at us. He's trying to smile like a film star.

'Here's my friend,' said Margaret. And she gave me a shove towards the boy on the pillion.

'Has she got a tongue?' Frank asked.

'A tongue! Did you hear that?' said Margaret, laughing and winking at me.

'Henri, give Mags your helmet, and then we'll leave you two in peace,' said Frank.

'You needn't go,' I said sheepishly.

But away they went, and before I knew where to turn I was in Henri's arms, my head out of sight in his armpits. And I'd have stayed there all the time, even though his coat was coarse and smelled, like someone's breath in the morning. But in a while he asked, 'What about a kiss?' 'What about a kiss?' he said a second time, and put his thumb under my chin.

He had a red face and red hair and a voice that made you think of manure and pigs and muck-raking and the like.

'You're much too tall for me. I've got a crick in the neck,' I said, fed-up with his wet kisses.

'What about going to lie down in the fern?' he said.

Only lovers with bad intentions lie in the fern. 'We'll sit on the roadside,' I said.

And there we sat for I don't know how long without speaking or looking at each other.

'A motor bike's lovely,' Margaret said after the boys had turned for home. 'Would you like to have a go some time?'

'You were a long time,' I said, close to tears. 'I'd got tired of waiting for you.'

'You've got grass stains on your frock,' she said. 'Grass stains are difficult to get off. Your mother'll be raving when she sees it.'

Mam was in the wash-house, carrying hot water from the boiler and was in a lather of sweat.

'Where have you been, girl?' she asked, though she couldn't see anything through the steam.

'Only for a walk,' I said, 'only for a walk.'

Out of a descended generation

labouring at sixteen,
Austin Healey Sprite at eighteen
by the ruined harbour warehouses.

Then Fridays, Whitbread by the crate
overrunning the counter:
pints downed in under ten seconds,
a record of seventeen pints a night.

The construction boom paid for it
and left Amlwch high and dry after five years:
the power station fully automatic
the unemployed in the white light
of a sunlit empty square

boys that went to school together:

one, pointed out to all comers across the years
in the reflected glory of a month
on bass for Rory Storm and the Hurricanes
with Ringo Starr in the early days:
he leaned against a wall,
rarely spoke but watched the buses leave,
had a small family at home, and a guitar;
others, footballers, of the only privileged class
(apart from the managers and shopkeepers
with their tenners and wives in the cocktail bars)
the real heroes of the school to the kids of the tribe
their Saturday blazers and clean,
greased hair to be emulated
who treated the teachers with a gangling negligence
protected little selected kids,
abandoned others to the pack
and joined to ostracise with irrelevancy
the smooth-collared English
who talked of being graded with their parents' approval
and left at the first opportunity.

But big Wyn, with his glazed baby eyes,
being chased round the cloakroom by the other kids,
punched in the balls, doubled up
never losing his fixed smile
a target for the smallest fish of all
his arms flapping with distress

big Wyn sweeps the roads –
all have a kind word for him.

Steve Griffiths: 'Anglesey Material'

Hay-making in Capel Gwyn

That was the day
we turned seven acres of hay
by hand.

Don't remember why, now –
                maybe
the little grey Fergie broke down.

Just the boys and me and that June blue morning
and those lines of felled grass lying
like love-maids' cut yellow tresses.

I had a two-pronged fork
and worked the left-hand stretch of field,
the warm-wood handle worn too smooth for spelks.

However heavy my step started,
I soon grew light in the sun, liked
the near-sounds my movements made:

the clean slip of steel, the sometimes scrape
on stone, the rustle of the cut-grass strands
showing
      a still-green underside.

Fiona Owen

Pigeon Feathers
a short story by Dewi Roberts

'I've got the finest pigeons in Wales, mun,' beamed Uncle George as he cupped one of his soft-bellied fantails in his large, work-soiled hands. 'In't she lovely?'

'Yes,' responded Jonathan touching the birds head gently in the semi-darkness of the warm loft. The other bright-eyed birds watched them keenly and made satisfied cooing sounds.

'These beauties are my pride and joy. A lot of men kept pigeons up the valleys when I was young. You can see why cant you?'

He gazed tenderly at his birds before stepping into the garden which lay behind the long, whitewashed cottage. The man and boy walked slowly into the kitchen and took their seats for dinner, which was being served with sullen indifference by Auntie Mair, Jonathan's great-aunt. She was a very thin woman of seventy who wore a permanent expression of anxiety on her face. She seldom, if ever smiled and always dressed very drabbly in clothing which looked as though it had been obtained at third hand from a charity shop. She spoke only when necessary, conversation being merely a means to an end.

But her husband was everyone's friend and enjoyed engaging total strangers in conversation, for many tourists found their way to this corner of Anglesey in the summer months. He was a bear of a man and wore suitably large clothing, usually a pair of very old ex-army khaki trousers and a much soiled tweed jacket. If he created the impression that he was pleased with the world then this was largely because of his fantails and the pleasure which they brought him. Auntie Mair had no time for the birds, and would often rant on about 'those damn old pigeons'.

They had met on a grey market day in Llangefni over thirty years ago and there was something about his solid, protective appearance which drew her to him. But the years had eroded the smooth edges of their marriage and this had now become a matter of habit and tolerance rather than effection and warmth. He had come up from the Rhondda to work in Holyhead port and his outgoing attitude proved popular with his workmates.

This was Jonathan's third Summer visit to the cottage and he enjoyed exploring the local countryside and, now that he was twelve, was allowed the freedom to go alone.

He would spend warm August days walking along the coastal footpath between Trefadog and Church Bay, a route which took him above some very high cliffs which towered above the sea far below. He would stop at various points, take out his binoculars and gaze intently at the oyster-catchers as they rode on the crest of the waves. He would seek out interesting driftwood like a seasoned beach-comber. Last year he had found the decomposed remains of a dolphin which, even in death, seemed to be wearing a smile on its face.

At the end of the day he would sit in the garden with Uncle George and was only too pleased to give a full account of what he had done and seen because he knew that this large, kindly man was really interested.

'I'll take you up on Carmel Head one day,' he told the boy, 'You get a good view of the Skerries from there.'

Uncle George enjoyed visiting the pub three times a week and, apart from anything else, it gave him the opportunity to discuss fan-tails with Eifion Lewis, another pigeon-fancier.

One evening he was sitting watching *Wales Today* and when it was over got up from his chair, stretched himself and announced that he was off to the pub for a drink. Auntie Mair's response was sudden and violent.

'And don't you never come back, you old sod' she shouted. 'Go on. Get out of my sight.'

Uncle George stormed out, slamming the door behind him.

Auntie Mair stood as though in a trance, the muscles of her face twitching.

'I want you in bed in ten minutes' she told Jonathan angrily. 'The last thing I want is a boy around my feet.'

Normally he did not go to bed during the Summer holidays until half past nine or ten.

When he got up to the small bedroom, facing the sea, he had already decided that he would not sleep that night. He got one of his *Star Wars* books from his hold-all and tried to read, but soon found that he could not concentrate.

When half past ten arrived he settled down and closed his eyes. But he kept seeing the image of Aunty Mair's angry face as it had revealed itself earlier and hearing her harsh words in his head. Eventually sleep must have enveloped him.

He was woken suddenly at two in the morning by the sound of angry voices. He sat up in bed, his heart thumping, and listened.

'You've damn well made a fool of me' Auntie Mair shrieked. 'You and that damn harlot of yours!'

'No woman, you're wrong,' protested Uncle George. 'I haven't been there, woman. I've been with Eifion. Ask him if you don't believe me.'

'You pig. Go on, get out of my sight.'

'Steady on the boy will hear.'

'A fine example you are to that boy. Get out, you sod.'

The front door was opened, and just as suddenly slammed shut again. Jonathan leapt out of bed, peered through the window and saw Uncle George striding purposefully down the garden path. A minute or so later he heard his Ford van starting up, and saw it move off until it had disappeared along the narrow, twisty road which led towards Llanfaelu.

After that Jonathan heard every hour strike on the sonorous grandfather clock in the kitchen downstairs. He had a knot of fear in his stomach and wanted nothing more than to be safely at home in his own bed in Chester. Sleep proved impossible after that and he tossed restlessly for the rest of the night.

Auntie Mair was usually up first at about seven o'clock, but there was no sound of activity on this particular morning. Jonathan could contain himself no longer and, in a mood of deepening anxiety, dressed quickly, opened his bedroom door and descended the stairs. The kitchen was deserted.

'Auntie' he called out, his voice trembling slightly. 'Auntie,. are you there?' There was no response and the only sound he could hear were the cries of scavenging gulls as they circled around the cottage.

He then went quickly upstairs again and knocked on Auntie Mair's bedroom door. When there was no response he opened it slowly and went in. The room was empty and the bed had not been slept in. He went downstairs again and, opening the front door, stepped out into the garden. What he saw immediately made him freeze. It was a scene of devastation that took his breath away.

The bloody corpses of all the fan-tails lay scattered in every corner of the small garden. Their throats had been cut and the bodies and heads lay strewn across the lawn. The force of the attack had caused feathers to fly in all directions and blood lay on the ground.

Uncle George stood by the loft, his faced creased in an expression of misery.

'It's a terrible wrong she's done me lad' Uncle George said. Tears were on his cheeks. 'What am I going to do?'

Jonathan walked over to him and without speaking a word they hugged each other. They remained in this embrace for a long time, or so it seemed to both of them. As they did so the clouds began to clear and a blustery gust of wind blew unexpectedly from the sea and scattered the feathers.

A Keepsake from Miss Adams

It lies heavy on the window sill,
Paperless, redundant since her death,
Its cold weight a memory of fly-away papers
Light and crisp,
Silenced and stilled.
'Know your place,' the age would say.

Like the furniture, like the fashion,
Its heavy feel depresses. Today we neatly
Clip and file in
Air-conditioned, breezy rooms.
Yesterday, they laboured slow to
Heavy ticking hours – and yet
That picture in the smooth glass mound
Adds interest, colour:
The carter with his load, the lumbering shire,
The Straits, the mountains, and of course the Bridge –
Britannia, towering above Victoria's waves.

How many stared and dreamed the lengthy hours
So many years ago into that scene,
Among the drapes and hangings, thick and dark?

The sunlight glints upon the polished glass.
The wistfull glance is gone; release at last.

Wendy Lloyd Jones

Gratitude

I can see the snow-capped Carneddau from my window and the Menai
below and there are primroses, violets, celandines and cowslips in the
lane. How wonderful it is to be able to walk with Megs to see them once
more! I am so very grateful.

From a letter written by octogenarian Teresa Francis: April 1998

Titles of interest about Anglesey

ANGLESEY – AN ISLAND'S STORY
Michael Senior
ISBN: 0-86381-389-5; £2.75

ANGLESEY SKETCHES
Margaret Hughes; illustrations by N. Squire Johnson
ISBN: 0-86381-540-5; £3.95

ANGLESEY PAST AND PRESENT
Wendy Hughes
ISBN: 0-86381-560-X; £4.95

TWO BRIDGES OVER MENAI
Robin Richards
ISBN: 0-86381-387-9; £2.75

CIRCULAR WALKS ON ANGLESEY
Dorothy Hamilton
ISBN: 0-86381-478-6; £4.50

SHROUDED QUAYS – THE LOST PORTS OF WALES
Aled Eames
ISBN: 0-86381-197-3; £2.50

THE HERRING FISHERS OF WALES
Mike Smylie
ISBN: 0-86381-467-0; £3.75

AN ANGLESEY ANTHOLOGY
Dewi Roberts
ISBN: 0-86381-566-9; £4.95

Full catalogue and price list available from:
GWASG CARREG GWALCH,
12 Iard yr Orsaf, Llanrwst, Conwy, Wales, LL26 0EH.

Walks with History

If you want to experience the very best of Wales, then these are the books for you. The walks are graded and there is something for everybody – short walks for families and more demanding routes to satisfy even the most experienced hillwalker.
Whether you choose to walk the high grounds, explore the beautiful valleys, study the varied wildlife or visit the remains of ancient castles and forts, the points of interest will explain what makes each area unique and help you choose the right walk for you.

Walks on the Llŷn Peninsula
PART 1 - SOUTH & WEST – N. Burras & J. Stiff.
ISBN 0-86381-343-7; **£4.50**
This series combines walks with history, stories and legends. Pastoral walks as well as coastal & mountain panoramas.

Walks on the Llŷn Peninsula
PART 2 - NORTH & EAST – N. Burras & J. Stiff.
ISBN 0-86381-365-8: **£4.50**

Walks in the Snowdonia Mountains
– Don Hinson. 45 walks, mostly circular, 96 pages, inc. accurate maps and drawings. 96pp ISBN 0-86381-385-2; New Edition: **£3.75**

Walks in North Snowdonia
– Don Hinson. 100km of paths to help those wishing to explore the area further. 96pp ISBN 0-86381-386-0; New Edition: **£3.75**

New Walks in Snowdonia
– Don Hinson. 43 circular walks together with many variations. This book introduces you to lesser known paths and places which guide book writers seem to have neglected. Maps with every walk. Pen & ink drawings. 96pp ISBN 0-86381-390-9; New Edition; **£3.75**

Circular Walks in North Pembrokeshire
– Paul Williams, 14 walks, 112 pages. ISBN 0-86381-420-4; **£4.50**

Circular Walks in South Pembrokeshire
– Paul Williams, 14 walks, 120 pages. ISBN 0-86381-421-2; **£4.50**

From Mountain Tops to Valley Floors
Salter & Worral. ISBN 0-86381-430-1; **£4.50**
Detailed information for casual/family walks and for the more adventurous walker.

NEW FOR 1998:
Circular Walks in the Brecon Beacons National Park;
ISBN 0-86381-476-X; **£4.50**
Circular Walks on Anglesey; ISBN 0-86381-478-6; **£4.50**
Circular Walks in Gower; ISBN 0-86381-479-4; **£4.50**
Circular Walks in Central Wales; ISBN 0-86381-480-8; **£4.50**
Circular Walks in Gwent; ISBN 0-86381-477-8; **£4.50**

WALKS IN WALES - latest titles

Walks from Llandudno
CHRISTOPHER DRAPER
ISBN: 0-86381-559-6; £4.95

Circular Walks in Meirionnydd
DOROTHY HAMILTON
ISBN: 0-86381-545-6; £4.50

Walks in and around the Berwyn Mountains
JOHN TRANTER
ISBN: 0-86381-547-2; £4.50

Circular Walks in North Eastern Wales
JIM GRINDLE
ISBN: 0-86381-550-2; £4.50

The North Wales Path and 10 selected walks
DAVE SALTER & DAVE WORRALL
ISBN: 0-86381-546-4; £4.50

Llŷn Peninsula Coastal Walks
RICHARD QUINN
ISBN: 0-86381-574-X; £4.50

Circular Walks in the Black Mountains
NICK JENKINS
ISBN: 0-86381-558-8; £4.50

Walks in the Wye Valley
RICHARD SALE
ISBN: 0-86381-555-3; £4.50